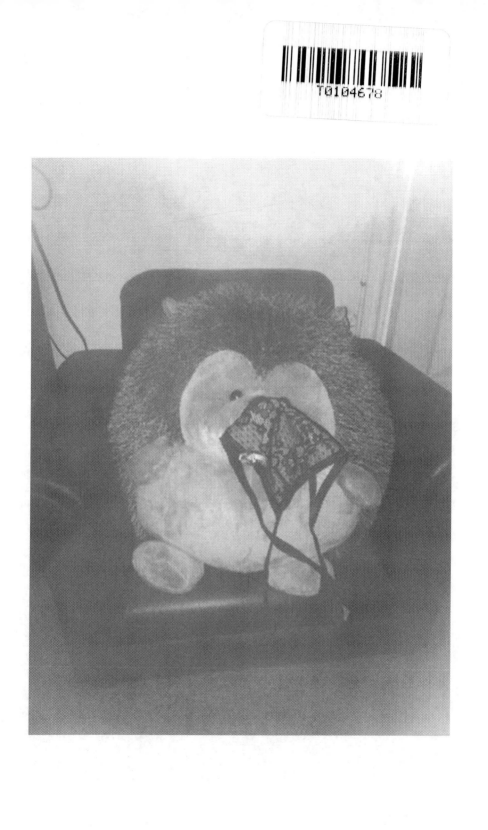

Dirty Sex Rainbows

The Autorhymeography Part 3

DARNEL SANCHEZ

AuthorHouse™ *UK Ltd.*
1663 Liberty Drive
Bloomington, IN 47403 USA
www.authorhouse.co.uk
Phone: 0800.197.4150

Published by AuthorHouse   06/05/2014

ISBN: 978-1-4969-7729-8 (sc)
ISBN: 978-1-4969-7728-1 (hc)
ISBN: 978-1-4969-7730-4 (e)

Contents

Again and Again 3

I said it in my first book
And in my second one
And I'm saying it again in my third
Again and again
Are both the same word
But if you want it to rhyme
With Ben, men or ten
You have to pronounce it like this
You have to pronounce it a-gen
However if you want it to rhyme
With words like Jane, pain or brain
Pronounce it as follows
Pronounce it a-gain!!!

Rik Clay What Did He Say?

In my last book 'Fifty Feels of Fuzz'
I went off on one about David Icke and lizard spies
And I'm aware based on the normal smut I write
How that might have taken some people by surprise
But I am completely honest when I write
So I couldn't exclude it, I just couldn't
I hoped some people would believe what I wrote
Although I was certain most people wouldn't
But I was obsessed, I was bang on the case
I'd spent a long time exploring the internet for clues
I'd spent months and months fishing on You Tube
For information and alternate fucking news
You name it I watched it
Everything to do with conspiracies and cover ups
The more I saw the more things sucked
Like a big tub of Chupa Chups
The Illuminati, the New World Order
Child sacrifices, the monarchy
Planet X, G.M.O's
It was all a bit too much for me
Hidden subliminal symbols everywhere
Main stream news pushing the agenda
Trying not to go nuts was proving well ard
Like that dog the ex Eastender
But I managed to hold it together
Fuck Jack Nicholson I handled the truth
I'd seen a human turn reptilian
Unfortunately I had no fucking proof
So in Fifty Feels of Fuzz I put it out there
I shared my problem with my readers to dilute it
Didn't want the entire weight of the world on my shoulders
It's too heavy, plus it smells cos cunts pollute it!
Anyway I need to rewind back in time
To early 2012 around May

To something I left out of my last book
Which was me hearing an interview with Rik Clay
You can still find it on YouTube
Just search Rik Clay Olympics 2012
He died a few weeks after doing that interview
And that fact made me want to delve
Deeper into what he'd researched
It was clear he had one hell of a brain
During his interview on Red Ice Radio
The Information he shared was insane
He had found out things about the forthcoming Olympics
And discovered things cloaked in mystery
The fucked up stuff he'd figured out
He legitimised with facts from history
Rik Clay was the first person to notice
That the London 2012 logo spelt out zion
Two weeks after doing the interview
He supposedly fell into a river whilst he was high on
L.S.D but if you hear his interview
You'll realise that he was articulate and bright
Something about the series of events
Just didn't seem quite right
But yeah that bloody Rik Clay interview
Rebooted my paranoia levels back up to max
He'd predicted a disaster at the London games
And I just couldn't fucking relax
During the build up to the Olympics
I was going crazy on my Facebook page
I was convinced something bad would happen
So I tried my hardest to engage
With people and convince them too
That shit was about to get real
This was back when I was banging Tufts
And in no way did she feel
The same as me about the Olympics
She thought I was a paranoid loon
She didn't believe in lizard people
Or aliens living on the moon

And this was all just before the point in my life
Where my last book abruptly ended
Thus this is where this book begins
For this was the exact time that I befriended
The bestest dominatrix in the world
Mistress Slaps the sassy crass hot diva
Maybe she'd be open minded like me
Perhaps she'd be a fucking reptoid believer!!

It All Began With A Squishy Fish Kiss

I don't know where it came from
Perhaps I was now officially demented
But by typing) and l and l and l and'
And < and—and—and X
The squishy fish kiss was invented
)lll'<—X

Mistress Slaps

If you use Facebook like a dating site
It's possible you might have some success
A lot of the time girls turn me down
But occasionally some say yes
Yes to actually meeting up with me
Yes to a drink or meal perhaps
So I sent a squishy fish kiss
To a lady whose name was Mistress Slaps
I'd actually sent out other squishy fish kisses
But it was only Slaps that took the bait
She loved her squishy fish kiss
She thought that it was great
So I invited her up to Whitstable
For dinner at an Italian restaurant called Zizzi
When you're armed with squishy fish kisses
Pulling birds online is easy!
Now I gotta say this Slaps lady
Well the photos on her Facebook page were kinky
Like the one of her in a Catwoman outfit
I bet when she took that off her cunt was stinky
There were other naughty pictures
And she looked fit in every one
She looked like a very naughty lady
And a whole shitload of fucking fun
So I was happy she'd agreed to come for a meal
And on the evening of it I waited keenly
Mistress Slaps looked like a porno bird
And I don't even mean that meanly
At about 7.30 pm she arrived
In her fucking lovely Audi
"Hello Fuzz" said Mistress Slaps
"Slaps you're here, howdy
Let me get your bag for you!"
I brought her bag inside

Mistress Slaps looked smoking hot
And her car was one classy ride
But Slaps had something about her
That made me suspect she was a whore
I don't mean a whore like just a slag
Those sluts tend mostly to be poor
No, Missy Slaps was doing well for herself
Hmm perhaps she was a brass
Not that that thought bothered me
I was too busy staring at her peachy arse
It was seriously peachy
Yum yum yum yum yum
Naughty face, amazing legs
And a nie on perfect bum!
Anyway we went to Zizzi for our Italian meal
Our conversation other diners I think found shocking
Slaps was one perverted hoe
Who I now wanted badly to stick my cock in
She revealed she was a dominatrix
And told me some of the stuff she had to do
Stuff that was almost unbelievable
Although she assured me it all was true
She said she's always upfront about her line of work
But that after hearing it most guys tend to do a runner
Not me! No way! I was in love
I mean what the fuck could be funner
Than dating a dominatrix
One that was into even more filthy shit than me
(Remember folks this is just the beginning
Of 'Dirty Sex Rainbows' the Autorhymeography Part 3)
We went back to my house after the meal
And snogged and kissed a lot
Mistress Slaps had promised her daughter she'd be home
Although she wished now that she had not
Cos Slaps was horny and so was I
Together serious sexual energy was being generated
But Slaps still left before we had sex
A decision I accepted but sure hated!

Darnel sanchez

My second date with Slaps went well
We went to the wine bar and drank two bottles of good pinot
Slaps was looking fit and I thought fucking this bitch
Would be like a big win up the casino
But I was also thinking that just maybe
I'd bitten off more than I could chew
Slaps was a full time dominatrix after all
And I was concerned as to what the crazy bitch might do
To me in the bedroom
I mean I'm just a pervy ball of fuzz
Maybe the fact I felt intimidated
Was part of the fucking buzz . . . .
So yeah we went back to my house
We kissed passionately there was chemistry for sure
I was looking forward very much now
To sticking my cock inside this whore
But when we got into bed
Well the nerves, they took effect
Slaps looked awesome naked
But my dick was not erect
I had to apologise "Sorry Slaps
For this anxiety I think I'm intimidated
My dick works fine normally
It was hard this morning when I masturbated
Perhaps I just need a piss
My cock will work fine after I've peed
I'll take a piss, roll a joint
My nerves will settle down if I smoke weed"
So that is what I did, I had my piss
Rolled a spliff and quickly smoked it
Went back to bed, licked Slaps minge
Spat on it and poked it!
I started to get erect
So Slaps sucked my cock until it went stiff
I was ok now, not panicking
Thanks largely to having smoked that spliff
Then we started fucking
Slaps was great to fuck, absolutely no doubt

8

I kissed her and sucked her ears
Whilst my dick went in and out
I started to probe her arse hole
I couldn't wait to fuck her arse
Birds this happy to be butt fucked
Are in all fairness pretty sparse!
I stuck it in her bum hole
To start with I was gentle
But once I'd built up rhythm
I went full thrust fucking mental!
I bummed Slaps like I had been possessed
By some demonic dark evil force
Did Slaps like this bumming from hell?
Damn right she did of course!
I bummed her with her legs up in the air
I bummed her doggy style and from the side
Every bumming position in the bum sex book
I think at some point in the night I tried
Yes this was a good sex session
And this was on our first night in bed together
We hadn't even started on the sex toys
Strap ons, pvc, whips, chains and leather!
I could see potentially we could be an awesome team
I was perverted so was she
Whatever filth I wanted to do to her
She wanted to do it back twice as bad to me
The possibilities were endless
But how far would I be prepared to go
Could I really be in a long term relationship with a woman
Who for all intents and purposes was still basically a hoe . . . .
Maybe I could, maybe not
Slaps was a very special creature
Sexy eyes, down to earth, amazing legs
But clearly her best feature
Was her enchanting talking arse hole
That thing was quite outstanding
It could talk to me "Pffftt rssp poppop pop"
Which when translated means "Thank you for the pounding!"

I liked Slaps very much
But I was in love with her peachy bum
As soon as I saw that thing
I just wanted to fill it full of cum
Slaps loved my pervy nature
She embraced my wrongness for what it was
She really fucking liked me
And she said it was basically because
I weren't the usual lairy geezer
The big gangster caveman trying to be tough
I was a funny pervy fuzz ball
Obsessed with arseholes, tits and muff
I wasn't put off by her line of work
Around me she could relax
She could tell me all about her day
Filling men's arseholes full of wax
Turning them into human candles
Pissing into men's ears
Kicking politicians in the nuts for cash
Reducing barristers to tears . . . .
She knew that I was ok with that
So long as she didn't do that shit to me
If rich business men wanted to pay to be humiliated
Then I really could not see
A problem with Slaps making money
Satisfying all those weirdos fetishes and kinks
Plus it gave us something to talk about
Whilst we sat in wine bars drinking drinks
Which we did a lot over the next few months
As a warm up to our nights of anal lust
We had a good relationship you see
Based on filthy sex and trust
And that's basically the introduction
To this Mistress Slaps period of time
Which means this is an ideal point to end this chapter
And officially welcome you to "Dirty Sex Rainbows"
The third and final part of my autobiography
Told entirely in rhyme!!

Craig

I have a little nephew Craig he's called
Although he's not little any more
See apparently, well actually
When he was around the age of four
And I was seven or maybe eight
I would fart on his head for fun
I doubt that he appreciated
Having to deal with the vibrations of my bum
But now he's six foot something
He's handsome, strong and tall
Perhaps the nutrients from my backside
Helped him to grow and not be small
So Craig feel free to thank me
Feel free to contact me to say
How me constantly farting on your head
Made you into the big fine man you are today!

Notorious P.I.G.

Not content with my dogs head gimp mask
I bought a new mask even more obscene
A fucking pigs head mask oink oink
Not streaky bacon fucking lean
Yes my pigs head mask is proper nasty
In bitches it really installs fear
They don't seem to want to wear it
And I keep making a right pigs ear
Of convincing them to do so
They say "No" no matter how kind I ask
"Not fucking no fucking yes you dirty pig
Shut up and put on the pigs head mask!"

Ham

One girl actually wore the pig mask
But she removed it as her piggy cunt I started to ram
Still I got to fuck her like it for a bit
Wham bam thank you Ham!!

The Electrocution Butt Plug

I was looking on a sex toy website
For a sex toy to use on Slaps
But what I chose to fucking buy
Could be seen by many as a judgement lapse
See I decided to buy a butt plug
But not a standard rubber one
No I decided to purchase an electrocution butt plug
Even though it cost a ton
£80 fucking quid it cost
But it looked seriously different class
And I knew Slaps wouldn't be opposed
To letting me pop it in her arse
So I made the online payment
Then told Slaps the awesome news
"I've bought an electrocution butt plug
Actually it has a warning 'do not use
If you suffer from high blood pressure
Or if you have a dodgy ticker'
And that's why you have to try it first Slaps
You bi sexual fanny licker!!"
A few days later in the morning
I was with Slaps at home in bed
When the postman knocked on my door
Normally I'd have ignored him but this time I instead
Jumped out of the covers
And down my stairs I quickly flew
See I didn't need to guess what he had
For I already fucking knew
It was the Electro Stim Electrocution Butt Plug
And Slaps was here oh joy
It meant I could get to see the power
Of this expensive shiny chrome arsehole toy
Slaps looked a bit uneasy
She didn't want to be fried like an inmate on death row

I on the other hand was like a kid at Christmas
And couldn't wait to use it on my hoe
But much to my annoyance
When I unpacked the fucking thing
It occurred to me that it did not have the capacity
To electrocute Slaps ring
It was just a solid chrome butt plug
With two holes in its base for wires
They didn't say it needed a control device
The fucking dirty liars
So I read the manual that was inside the box
And discovered I needed a power pack
Which cost another £90 pound
I shoulda sent the damn thing back
Instead I ordered the power grid
Slaps for now was off the hook
But a few days later and I had it
Which is why this rhyme made the book
The first night I used it on Slaps
Was an interesting affair
I popped it in her bottom
But Slaps is hard core and didn't care
So I turned the power up a notch
From green to red on the power gage
I turned it up to full throttle
Then unleashed some sexual rage
I fucked Slaps hard and rubbed her clit
Whilst the butt plug zapped away inside her shitter
The pleasure from its intense pulsations
Had now clearly hit her
She was getting fucking vocal
I felt bad for Chris trying to sleep
As I kept the butt plug in her butt
Whilst ramming my cock in her pussy ball bag deep
Slaps liked the toy I chose to buy
She came a lot that night, she sure did
And as well she should the lucky bitch
That pleasure she felt in her arse cost me £200 quid!!

Boar

I put the pig mask on to fuck Slaps
The dominatrix whore
But due to all my fucking fuzz
I looked like a wild boar!!

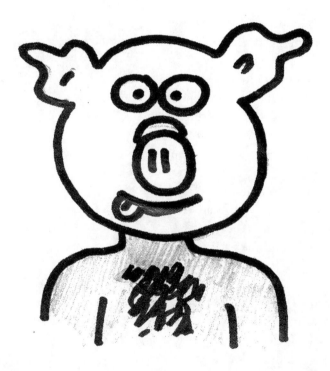

Fiddy Cent

Back in my Scottish Power days (2007)
I had the joy of working with my pal Trevor
And one day during this time he decided
To do something out of the blue and very clever
He announced to Matt and I that he had bought tickets
For us to all see Fiddy Cent at the Hammersmith Apollo
When it comes to random surprises
This one from Trev will certainly be hard to follow
Anyway we all mugged off work early
Cos the tickets were for that same night
"We should buy some drugs" said Matt
"Yes Matt my friend I think you're right!"
So we went and got some E's and weed
Should I admit that? Ha I don't care one fucking iota
Everyone's on fucking drugs and so were we
On the way up to London in Trev's motor
"It gets even better boys!" said Trev
"I've also booked us a local hotel . . . .
It's literally around the back of the Apollo
Wait til you see it, I've done well"
But when we got there it looked like a church
It had stained glass windows and a cross
Not that Matthew or myself
Really gave much of a toss
As we entered, in the lobby
There was a vicar sat at an organ playing
Still never mind we had a room with three beds
On which later we'd happily be laying . . . .
So we checked in, went to our room
Built a joint and crushed some E's
Smoked the joint, sniffed the pills
Should we have felt bad doing it in a house of Jeez
Uz? Well sorry but there's nothing about drug taking
In the Bible Old Testament or New

So we rolled more joints to take with us
Then decided the next thing we should do
Would be to go queue up in the queue
May as well get in as early as we could
Tim Westwood was the warm up D.J.
And his D.J. sets are pretty good
So we left our Christian base camp
Went down to the Apollo but didn't fancy queuing
Instead we walked right past the massive line
The queue looked pissed off like what you fuckers doing
Well I'm not sure how but we walked straight in
And were soon drinking at the bar but we weren't smoking
Cos this was the day after the smoking ban came into effect
Not smoking at a Fiddy Cent concert you must be joking
Fuck the rules fuck the system
We had three joints pre rolled and stashed
Obviously we planned to smoke them
We'd been sniffin E's and we were mashed!
Right lets fast forward to the moment
When Fiddy Cent hit the stage and started rappin
Cos this was when we sparked joint number one
Which caused some dudes near us to start clappin . . . .
We were the first people to blaze a J
But soon other people followed suit
Still feel kinda proud though that out of that crowd
We were the first to have the balls to spark a zoot
I think Fiddy was mid-way through
Window Shopper or P.I.M.P.
When Trevor handed another stinky spliff
Sneakily to me!
I had a couple of big tokes
Then passed it on to Matt
However unbeknown to Matt or me
Was the fucking fact that
A security guard was right behind us
And had clocked the bifta in Matts hand
He grabbed us both and marched us out
Saying you know indoor smoking's just been banned

And just like that Matt and I
Found ourselves outside feeling silly
Outside was no fun at all
It was dark and glum and chilly
We walked away from the Apollo
Whilst debating our next move
Coming to the conclusion that if you don't try
You won't succeed and that point we sure did prove
We swapped coats and took off our caps
Turned around, we could get back in again
Maybe the security wouldn't realise
That we were the same two men . . . .
That they had just kicked out
Yes we had planned precisely our stealthy mission
See we still had our fucking tickets
And even though they stated clearly no re-admission
We reckoned we could blag it
And when the security said no re-admittance
We explained that when we went to buy drinks inside
We only had in cash a tiny pittance
But the barman was not accepting card
And told us to go get cash from a cash point
(Fortunately the security at the door were not aware
We'd recently been evicted having been caught smoking a joint)
So yeah we explained we'd been to get some more cash
So they saw sense and let us in
We hurriedly dashed back into the crowd
Both sporting giant cheesy grins
Trev was where we'd left him
He weren't missing Fiddy for nuffin so he stayed
He was very impressed though
With the bare faced cheek me and Matt displayed
Now the fact we'd almost missed seeing Fiddy Cent
Made being there to see him even better
I mean just writing about it right now
Is making me smile more with every letter
It could have been so tragic
But it was cool it was a blast

I love remembering funny shit like this
When writing about stories from my past . . . .
Once Fiddy was finished we went back
To our churchy hotel type of place
I felt a wee bit sinful though
Going back there off my face
Never the less we still skinned up in the hotel room
Then went outside to smoke the green
Which was when we saw Fiddy and his crew
In their stretch humma limousine
See our church slash hotel
Was located on a tiny secluded back street
Which Fiddy's limo driver I'm assuming
Had decided as an exit option was discreet
But what he could not have envisioned
Was the car blocking up this narrow road
It looked like the old man in the driver's seat
Was sat there waiting to be towed
The limo driver was shouting "Move it"
This old man had ruined the limo driver's sly escape
The old man then shouted something back
Which was when Fiddy wound down his window and began to tape
The funny shit that was happening on his phone
The funny shit was us
We were shouting "Fiddy what's up!! G-unit!!"
And he'd obviously decided to check out the noise and fuss
We were like "Yo Fiddy we'll make him move his car
How about we bust a cap in his old ass
Then jack his fucking motor and drive off
So your limousine can pass!!"
For about 10 minutes Fiddy was stuck in his limo
Right outside our place of faith
Until the old man started up his car
Man that old fool must have felt unsafe
With us E'd up hoodlums hurling abuse
And G-unit in their stretch hummer bibbing their horn
Poor old chap by the time he pulled away
He was looking fucking forlorn!

Darnel sanchez

We took some snaps of Fiddy and G-unit
As their limo finally got going
And they took some photos of us
Photos at some stage we hoped they might be showing
To their wacky gangster rapper friends
Photos of myself, Trevor and Matt!
Yo Fiddy that night you played Hammersmith Apollo
Was dope, crazy fucking phat!!!

Making Rainbows

Red and yellow and pink and blue
Have absolutely nothing to do
With the rainbows in this story
These rainbows are far more gory
See after bumming Slaps like a demon
Out of her arsehole would leak my semen
As well as bum gravy and pussy gunk
Hints of blood and left over spunk
That had only just found its way out
Now please be sure be in no doubt
There'd be traces of wee and poo in the trail
That Slaps left on my sheets like a slutty snail!

Dirty Sex Rainbows

Yes the trails on my white sheets
Were a sight to behold
Like dirty sex rainbows
But at their end there was no pot of gold
Just Slaps's gaping arsehole
Winking at me
The rainbows she made with her arse
Were things of stunning beauty
It was like magic
A miracle, a great work of art
We made wonderful rainbows together
I'd cum in Slaps's bum then she'd fart
Then the rainbow would appear
Cream, brown, blood red and yellowish mustard
Slaps's arse produced a rather strange
Sexually manufactured squirty bum custard
No other female, no other woman
No other girl that I've ever met
Has come close to Slaps's rainbows
And I can safely say it's a sure bet
That there will be no other lady
Able to make art with her arse like Mistress Slaps
No other has or will ever squirt out
Such magnificently artistic spunk ridden craps
All over my bed sheets
And in such a way it creates a rainbow effect
No other before her or after
Will be so keen to try to perfect
Using their arseholes
To paint dirty sex rainbows for me
Which is why Mistress Slaps
Will in my eyes always be

Much more than a companion
Much more than a friend
For she is a magical goddess
That can conjure up rainbows of wrongness
From out of her rear end!!!

Hedgehogs

I never got to meet either of my Grandads
But this poem starts with the one from my mother's side
Apparently once when he was digging in the garden
He skewered a baby hedgehog, then broke down and cried
Because he was by all accounts a sensitive man
My mum says he was caring and good hearted
Unfortunately I was only a year old
When from our world he departed
Although I'm thinking somehow he lives on in me
For I have always had an affinity with hedgehogs
I like them way more than polar bears
Rabbits, cats or big dogs
And every year on my birthday
One would come and visit me
Without fail from the age of five I think
My prickly friend would come and see
Little Pimpy on his birthday
Year after year without fail
I'm really sorry about what my Grandad did
He really didn't mean to impale
One of your hedgelings on his garden fork
I've been told himself for weeks on end he hated
In fact come to think of it maybe you are him in hedgehog form
Perhaps you are him re incarnated!!
I loved my special birthday hedgehog visits
I had lots of hedgehog soft toys, I still do!
Ok not lots that's an exaggeration
I actually just have two . . . .
A small one and a big fat one
He has his own flash leather chair
A hedgehog soft toy with his own lazy boy
Is really rather rare
But I have one in my bedroom
And he really likes to sniff

Darnel sanchez

Ladies dirty underwear
He loves a big ol' whiff
Of dirty thongs and knickers
So I try to insure any sluts I fuck leave theirs behind
I will hide them under my bed
Which is why in the morning they never find
Their dirty stinky underwear
It's a mystery they can't work out
Then once they've gone I retrieve them
And hang them on the end of my hedgehog's snout!!!

Bad Grandma

My mums mum, my Grandma is dead!
So I shouldn't say bad things about her
But I'm gonna what the heck
Cos the only memory I have of that ol' cunt
Was her hooking her walking stick around my neck!
If I have any lizard D.N.A.
It's definitely come from that nasty witch
I'm allowed to say this cos my mum also says
That my Gran was a right old bitch
So Gran if you can read this
You are a proper nosey ghost
I guess you live on in my D.N.A. too
Another voice in my head! Have I been a gracious host?
Oh fuck! Of course you're my vicious streak
My spitefulness that comes from you
Get out of my head you evil woman
You heard me, go on, shoo!!!

The 2012 Olympic Shames

As I told you at the start of this book
I was sure the Olympics would spell disaster
Getting to grips with this conspiracy shit
Was something I had yet to master
I'd already informed everyone on Facebook
That something monumentally bad was about to transpire
But nothing happened at the Olympics
Leaving me looking like a gullible brainwashed liar
However there was loads of subliminal imagery
The opening ceremony was an occultists fucking dream
Nothing at that demonic ritual
Was what it fucking seemed!
Still I eased up on my conspiracy preaching
And focused instead on the nice round baps
Of the lady who by now you're all familiar with
That filthy dominatrix Mistress Slaps!
See whilst the British Olympians won gold medals
I invented my own decathlon of sorts
Each event involved arsehole fucking
Far more fun than traditional mundane Olympic sports
I was giving Slaps the long hump
I was breast stroking her breasts like a winner
I was shooting my Usain Bolt
Whenever I stuck my pole vault in her
I scored maximum points in arserobics
I came first in synchronised rimming
My semen even formed a relay team
They came out my baton and started swimming . . . .
Yeah so basically what I'm saying
Is that I think Slaps and I deserve a few gold medals
Slaps rode my cock better than Bradley Wiggins rode his bike
And she didn't even need a handlebar or pedals
Not that I'd want to win gold for team G.B.
I feel less proud to be British every year

When it was the Queens Jubilee
I didn't wave a Union Jack or cheer
Don't get me wrong there was a time
When I was a loyal subject of the Queen
Now when I look at that evil bitch
I see something cold blooded, ruthless and mean!
I actually believe she is demonic
I'd be prepared to hold up a giant banner
Saying "Queen Elizabeth wants to eat your children
And she had the S.A.S. murder Diana!!"
There's something vile about the royals
Charles and Jimmy Savile they got on well
As far as I'm concerned all those lizard fucks
Can die and burn in hell!
In fact whilst I'm on this subject
Let me answer a question about the Pope
Is the Pope catholic? Yes of course!
Does that make him a good person? Nope!
He's another demonic fucktard
Head of the world's largest paedophile ring
Catholic priests like fucking little boys
They can't help it it's just their thing . . . .
It's like there's this one big giant network
Of sick twisted child molesters
Vicars, priests, celebrities, boarding school teachers
They're all a bunch of noncey Uncle Festers!
The BBC covered up Jimmy's antics
For fifty years they fixed it for him
Little boys and little girls
Even dead bodies got raped by Jim
And he was able to get away with it
Cos of his important friends
The police would tell the victims to shut up
His crimes reported to no ends
So you know what if this fucking offends you
In the mirror take a long look
If you're less offended by what Savile was allowed to do
Than you are by what I'm writing in this book

Then you've got questionable morals
What if your kid had been abused
But the police didn't fucking investigate
You'd be a bit confused
Until you found out it was cos Jim was in with the royals
And that meant he was untouchable unlike your kid!
Police Chiefs, BBC execs, his celebrity friends,
Everyone, they all knew what he did
But yet he never ended up in court!
You still wanna wave your Union flag
You still wanna bow down and curtsey
To Camilla Parker Bowles the dog faced slag? . . .
Fuck it I'm on one!
The whole thing fucking stinks
So I'm saying what I wanna say
I couldn't care less what people think!
I used to be proud to be British
God save our gracious Queen
There aint no God and the Queen aint gracious
Her wealth is unjust it's plain obscene
The commonwealth is a result of theifdom
The crusades continue they haven't stopped
The royal family still run the world
And I expect my head will end up chopped
Off for what I'm writing here
But the queen is a reptile I'm sure
She's a sadistic, un-empathetic, brutal
Child eating greedy whore!
The British Empire is the dark side of the force
The royal bloodline contains reptilian D.N.A.
Godzilla save the fucking Queen
Is what our national anthem should fucking say!
I don't want to be a royalist subject anymore
All you flag waving, bunting lovers go eat your cake
When your house gets repossessed ask yourself
What difference did your flag waving fucking make!
I'm pro peace, pro life, pro human
I know killing is not right

Darnel sanchez

I'd defend my loved ones I'd defend my friends
But personally I wouldn't go and fight . . . .
For Queen and fucking country
Send David Cameron and Tony Blair
They send our soldiers off to war
But don't go themselves that's hardly fair
At least in medieval times
The King would lead his men on the battlefield
Our last two Prime Ministers the smug spineless pricks
Would probably use children to fucking shield
Them from oncoming fire
The N.W.O. lizard loving fucks
The fact they get paid to fuck us over
Well it's bullshit man it sucks
And as for poor old Rik Clay
The guy who exposed dark Olympic undertones
Take a look at what he said
On your laptops and smartphones
Find his redice radio interview
So you can see what I'm on about
Maybe he got murdered
Cos he managed to work too much stuff out
Maybe what he exposed made them change their plans
Perhaps he spoke out just in time
And perhaps I'll be murdered once this book is out
For writing this controversial rhyme
"Off with his head he's a traitor!"
The Queen will say "That rhyme is an act of treason!"
Fuck it if I gotta die
At least it'll be for a damn good reason!!
The end (of me!)

Roll Up Roll Up

Roll up roll up
Stroke the magic chest of fuzz
50p a go if you want to know
What stroking my chest hair does!

Roll up roll up
Stroke my magic hairy chest
50p and you will see
The power of what's under my vest

Roll up roll up
Touch my magic fuzz for luck
50p a turn then you will learn
Why I'm such a lucky fuck!

Roll up roll up
Run your fingers through my fur
50p a try don't be shy
Once you've done it you'll concur
That my chest hair has magic power
It will bring you fortune, fame and wealth
Roll up roll up pay me 50p
And you can see for your fucking self!!

Roll Ups

Girls what are you doing
Digging around in a pouch of Amber Leaf
Rolling tobacco is rank
You look like a skank
And it stains your lovely white teeth!

Zoe

I love my sister Zoe
But I don't see her as often as I should
If I wasn't such a numpty
I'm sure I probably would
Maybe her teachery ways
Make me feel like I've been naughty
I'm pretty sure I'll go and see her more
When I'm around the age of forty!!

Sam

Sam is the youngest of Zoe's kids
He's quite outspoken and supports the yids
You never know what he's gonna say
No matter what, he says it anyway
Sam is Sam just let him be
He's quite unique and like me
In that I think he probably verges
On having borderline Asperger's!!!

Duck My Sick

Slaps was fucking awesome
She never neglected to suck my balls
Plus she would give herself home enemas
She was dedicated to the cause
No shit, nope, no bum gravy
Why? Cos she would always douche
Which is quite unusual
Like that programme 'The Mighty Boosh'
No other birds have had that kind of commitment
To getting their arseholes stuffed with dick
She wouldn't eat on the days she came to see me
And sometimes this meant she'd be sick
Cos as soon as she got to my house
We'd go to the wine bar for a tipple
Chris didn't need to be seeing me abuse her arse
Whilst simultaneously chewing her nipple
So I'd get out of my housemates way
Cos I knew he went to bed quite early
Which is when we'd return and I'd fuck Slaps in her divine brown
As if I was Hugh Grant cheating on Liz Hurley!
But yeah cos poor Slaps wouldn't have eaten
All the wine she'd consumed would make her pukey
Poor bitch would be fucking ill
Like that kid in the film New Jack City 'Pookie'
Now the first time this happened
Well I was a proper gentleman at first
She was on all fours throwing up in my toilet
This was Slaps looking her worst . . . .
So I held her hair up for her
And got her a glass of water
As she regurgitated all that fucking expensive wine
That I'd only recently just bought her
But see the thing is, Slaps bent over throwing up
Really made me want to hump her

Darnel sanchez

So I parted her lovely butt-ocks
She was my Jenny and I was about to Forest Gump her
So yeah I'm a bit perverted
But I had an erect dick
And I fucked Slaps from behind
Whilst she was keeled over being sick
Call me a wrongen all you want to
I surrender look I'm waving my white flag
I admit defeat I am a wrongen
But Slaps's vagina tightened with each gag!
I pulled out and cum all over her
Yes it's offensive but who knew
That Slaps vomiting in my bog
Would make my dick want to throw up too!!

Dirty Sick Ducker!

A few nights later Slaps was sick again
But this time I was less of a gentleman than before
I didn't even hold her hair up
I just smashed the fuck out of her backdoor
Yep whilst Slaps heaved into my crapper
I fucked her crapper and made it gape
Her misfortune made me horny
So her arsehole I had to rape
Poor Mistress Slaps I hear you say
Oh contraire she loved it
The more she yacked the harder my dick got
And the further in I shoved it!
So next time your girlfriend drinks too much
On a night out, gets in and begins to hurl
Don't just stand there nursing the drunken slut
Tell her she's been a naughty girl
Then pull her skirt above her head
And her panties to one side
And fucking fuck that puking slut
Go ahead stick your erection deep inside
Hold her hair up if you want to
I wouldn't bother, just let it get all sicky
Spit on her arse and call her a cunt
Really take the mickey
Then either fill her full of jizz
Or pull out and jizz into the bitches hair
Just make sure afterwards you ask her if she feels ok
And kiss her to show her you still care!!

Zo Zone

Back when I was fourteen or so
I'd often go to see my sister Zo
With Ian and Richard the speccy twat
And a kid called Gaybraham and the reason that
We'd go to see my sister was cos we could drink there
And my mum was ok cos she knew where
We were and that we were safe and warm
Getting pissed with Cheep and Orm!!

Orm and Cheep

My niece Laura fell down the steps
Holy moly Jesus wept!
My mum and sister had a cry
Laura had a big black eye
She was seeing birds tweet tweet tweet
Could have ended up in Great Ormand Street
Instead she ended up with Orm on her wall
Cos Zo and Phil thought it might be cool
If I were to draw big murals
Of Orms and Cheeps yes I'm using plurals!
Who are Orm and Cheep? I'll get you acquainted
Orm's a worm Cheeps a bird
I'm guessing of them you might not have heard
Well in the 80's they had their own cartoon show
Ok that's Orm and Cheep now you know!!!!

Liam

Liam is the middle one of Zoe's three
He now lives in Cornwall with Tracey
He's very happy living there
He's got great big floppy hair
He's a good lad, kind and nice
He's only got one major vice
His one misdemeanour, his one big sin
He gets drunk fast when he drinks Sloe Gin!!

Albert

Albert is almost 100 years old
He lives in London in a flat
He's very generous at Christmas time
And his best friend is a cat!!

Zoe's Phil

Rhymes about my sister Zoe's Phil
So far total zilcho nil
No rhymes about him would be too harsh
When you stop to consider his fine moustache!!

I Can't Believe It's Not Butt Sex!

Slaps invited me to her flat
Just for a bit of a change
It was something I'd been putting off
Cos I'd rather fuck in my own house than somewhere strange
But I could cope with one night at hers
It wasn't something that was gonna cause a row
Anyway that same day my daughter handed me a present
Which was a face mask of a farmyard cow
Moo! Moo! Moo! Moo! Moo! Moo!
Thank you kindly for my mask!
Just after that Slaps phoned and requested
I buy alcohol, a fairly simple task
But the cow mask got me on a milk vibe
Thus the alcoholic drink I fancied drinking
Was Malibu and ice cold milk
Now I know what you're all thinking
Malibu and milk that sounds disgusting
Well you might think that but
The ice cold milk mixed with Malibu
Only really tastes of milk and coconut
Which is lovely just like most of Kent
The garden of England and my home county
Alternatively you could use chocolate milk
And make liquid fucking Bounty!!
So armed with my Malibu and milk
I headed to Slaps's flat
I'd get to meet her lizard Barny
I was just glad it weren't a cat . . . .
Slaps cooked Mexican food for dinner
We got stoned and drank our coconut milk shake
Then went to bed and started having sex
But not long into it I stopped for a toilet break
Cos I needed a jimmy riddle
That's cockney rhyming slang

For needing a tiddle, taking a piss
Or to go and drain ones wang!!
But on the way to Slaps's lavvy
Out of the corner of my eye
I saw my cow mask in my holdall
I'd brought it with me fuck knows why
Then a thought popped into my head
It was messed up and quite crazy
I'd have my piss, put on the mask
Then go fuck Slaps whilst pretending to be Daisy!
I got back into bed with the cow mask on
Slaps said that I looked scary
I stuck my cock in her potty mouth
Lucky she's not intolerant to dairy!
I fucked her with the mask still on
I did things that were rude
Slaps called me a dirty cow
I moo'ed and moo'ed and moo'ed!
Then Slaps milked me for my creamy goodness
And told me that she thought I was a nutter
My cream went all over her face
"I can't believe that it's not butter"
Is what I said as it came out!
Slaps lapped it up, yes she said it was delicious
That's right I'm a big naughty cow
And my cum tastes udderlicious!!!

Slaps Straps On!

On the first date I had with Slaps
I told her that she could fuck me with a strap on
I didn't think for one minute
That was ever really gonna happen
But after a month or so of bumming Slaps
She decided it was her turn to administer some bummage
Truth is I was a scaredy scarecrow
A fucking frightened Worzel Gummidge!
I didn't really feel that comfortable
Letting this ruthless dominatrix loose on my botty
Not with a big black strap on
Fuck that shit I'm not potty
But she kinda backed me into a corner
So I said I'd let her have a go
I'd stuck things up my own arse
Never let no one else do it though
Unfortunately I couldn't relax and felt some remorse
For all the hoes I'd ever sodimised
And as for the hoes that fucking bottled it
Well with them I now empathised
Cos I didn't like it when the tip went in
I stopped Slaps and told her she couldn't do it
"You big fuzzy wimp" said Mistress Slaps
"I thought you wouldn't I just knew it!"
I told her I would need to be high or drunk
As this was an excuse I'd heard from many a bitch
Now I was in their position
This was a role reversal switch
Slaps wasn't happy with me at all
So I said she'd still get to do it just not then
At which point I took the strap on off of her
And said sorry but I guess it's your fucking turn again
Slaps had had her chance to bum rape me
But the opportunity had long since passed!

I took the dildo out of the leather strapping
Then buggered Slaps with it brutally and fast
I decimated her fucking bum hole
Whilst she rubbed her clit until she squirted
"I'm sorry you didn't get to do this to me!"
I said apologetically "But I was scared in case it hurted!"

Carrot Bum

When I was very young
I was rumbled by my mum
Sticking carrots up my bum
Sorry mum but I think you'll find
I liked sticking carrots up my behind
I know this played on your mind
So I'll take this opportunity to say
It wasn't cos I was gay
It was just that I hoped one day
I'd be able to see out my arse in the dead of night
That somehow the carrots would give my bum hole sight
Turns out I proved myself right
It worked! Don't believe me, go on give it a try
Trust me mum I wouldn't lie
I use my arsehole as my third eye
Hand on my heart I'm telling you
I know it's hard to believe but it's true
I can see from where I poo
I have 20/20 sight
From out the place I take a shite
What once was dark is now bright
So if you find your wayward son
Stinking carrots up his bum
Don't worry about it like my mum
Don't despair, don't throw a fit
In fifteen years he'll be able to see himself shit
It really works I've proven it
If definitely doesn't mean your son is gay
It just means he's found another way
To get one of his five a day

Darnel sanchez

You should embrace this carrot lark
Your son's actually a bright spark
He'll be able to pull down his pants to see in the dark
Finally to you this advice I lend
Be understanding be his friend
And buy him a new carrot for his rear end!!

YO!! MTV Slaps

Slaps said she wanted an apprentice
A young dominatrix she could train
So I found her an apprentice
Won't make that mistake again!
See the girl who I thought could be her trainee
Was a girl who loved my first book
She was the first person at my book signing
She poses nude and stuff and has a dominatrix look
So I asked her if it was something she'd considered
"Yes I've often thought about it" she replied
"Well my missus Slaps is a dominatrix and she's recruiting
I'll try and hook you up!" but soon I wished I'd never tried
Slaps had the fucking right arse
"She's a rat faced hoe how do you even know her?"
"She's just a mate that might like to be your understudy
I figured your talents you could show her!"
Slaps phoned her up anyway
Despite on her not being keen
But the nudey girl told Slaps she'd changed her mind
Which was when Mistress Slaps turned mean
She slagged off my little nudey fan
Then accused me of fucking cheating
I hadn't cheated on Slaps once
Humble fucking pie she should be eating
Slaps had a dark side she was bound to have
To not think that would be naïve
But now I was thinking she was almost
Behaving like a female Geordie Steve
Volatile when out in public
Able to cause confrontational situations out of nowhere
Other people, normal people, nice people
She would find it fun to scare
Plus cos she looked so naughty
She'd no doubt attract big baldy lairy twats

You know the doorman type
Pumped up arms covered in tats!
I don't like confrontation
Much like my sister Sadie
Slaps however loved it
She was just that kinda lady
But you see I know where confrontational behaviour leads
It leads to unpleasant confrontations
Angry doorman with rolled up sleeves
Sporting self-inflicted lacerations
Wanting to beat me up
Fuck that I don't like fighting
I'm a hedgehog I curl up into a ball
I'd rather stay in and do some writing
Slaps was fucking awesome though
The bigger the personality the bigger the risk
Do you wanna hear some Swedish?
Sla han ta hans fisk!
That's smack him take his fish in Swedish!
Sort of thing Slaps would've said is she were a Swede
Was this someone I could really be with?
Hmm some time to ponder on it I would need!!

Rita and Mumpy

Chris went on a dating site
The first woman he dated Rita
Sounded great in theory
Till I got to meet her
She looked like a sixty year old
Lunchtime school assistant
But Chris was determined to find love
Yes that boy is quite persistent
So when he found another bird on the dating site
He was proper over the moon
She was a dumpy mumpy kinda girl
Who you'll hear me mention again pretty soon!!

Rita

Chris oh Chris
I did not expect this
I can't believe that is Rita
I don't mean to attack her
But she is hardly a cracker
More of a crusty Rivita!!

Mumpy Rift

Chris was at his mums with his daughter
I had to go to work
Chris left Mumpy in his room
I left Slaps in mine 'beserk'
Cos what I'd over looked
Was Slaps massive dislike of Mumpy
Slaps was sassy and full of filth
Mumps was dull and frumpy
Slaps contacted me in the afternoon
She was getting vexed
"I'm gonna knock this fat cunt out!"
Were the words I think she text
Mumpy was swanning around like she owned the place
The big fat Mumpy fuck
This was Slaps home territory
And she was about to have a ruck
I phoned Slaps and calmed her down
But I could see Slap's point
Mumpy had made me feel uncomfortable
When she glared at me as I smoked a joint
This wasn't gonna work
Slaps was a bomb ready to explode
Mumpy had a pompous superior attitude
And her luck I think she rode
Slaps would have fucking killed her
Slaps would have weighed her in
She would have smashed the heel of her stiletto
Right into Mumpy's stupid deformed podgy grin
However as it happened things between me and Slaps
Were not all peaches and cream
And Mumpy was just another problem
In the Fuzzy Slaps dream team!!

A Slaps In Judgement

Slaps was everything sexual I'd ever wanted
All I could want for or desire
There was passion, there was filthiness
Sometimes our sex truly was on fire
But you know that old saying
You can have too much of a good thing
Well it had gotten to the point
Where I was taking for granted fucking Slaps's ring
Plus there was a problem
I liked Slaps but when it came to the crunch
Could I really be with her long term? Probably not!
Unfortunately Slaps wasn't stupid she had a hunch
That if she were to give me an ultimatum
To either be together properly or split
I'd back out of our relationship
But why would she do that? Ultimatums make things shit!
I dunno, women hey! They're a strange bunch
The logic to their thinking is a puzzle impossible to solve
"I want us to be together properly" said Slaps
"I want our relationship to evolve"
And there it was Slaps's ultimatum
Commit to something long term or I'm outtie!
"I can't do that I'm sorry!" I replied
Then Slaps got the hump and drove off in her Audi
I told her I knew I'd regret that decision
Probably for the rest of my life
I thought a lot of Slaps but I wasn't ready
To try and turn that hoe into a housewife
If Slaps hadn't forced my hand
What we had could've gone on much longer
Maybe after time my feelings for her
Would have become a little stronger

But at this stage I wasn't ready to commit
So Slaps told me I couldn't see her anymore
"Thanks a lot" said Slaps sarcastically as she left
"You've made me a dominatrix feel like a worthless whore!"

Pizza Ass

Slaps blamed me for her parking fines
Slaps called me a male slut
I missed helping myself to her arsehole
Like lunchtime buffet at Pizza Hut!
So I tried my best to keep things
Between me and Slaps friendly, polite and civil
Which was about as easy for me as it was
For Basil Fawlty when he attempted it with Sybil
(Back in that programme Fawlty Towers
An old sitcom set in a hotel)
Cos Slaps was cunting me off more than Brand and Ross
Cunted off Andrew Sachs the guy who in it played Manuel!!

I'll Slaps You With A Court Summons

"If you write about me in a book
Your life won't be worth living!"
Well I went and did it anyway
So I hope you feel forgiving!

Goldilocks

I knew long term I couldn't be with Slaps
What with her being basically a whore
Then one day whilst I was working in Dover
A young blonde girl answered her door
She was petite and had a pretty face
Not too bad for a Dover single mother
She was happy to do my survey
Which I did much like any other
But I was feeling confident
I'd been on a role all year
Whatever I visualised seemed to materialise
And I was visualising hanging out of this girl's rear
So I saved her number from the survey
The data protection act did not protect her data
I'm not stupid though and was careful in choosing
The text I texted her a little later
Couldn't go steaming in with something sexual
Like 'I think you're fit fancy a fuck?'
What if she reported me to head office
Well that'd be some real bad luck
Cos if she did I'd get sacked for sure
No more job for me
So instead I texted "thanks for doing my survey
I'm on Facebook under the name Darnel Pimpydee
If you were to be my Facebook friend
I could let you know when I'm doing a survey with an incentive
So yeah add me and I'll hook you up!"
When exploiting the data protection act you have to be inventive
Anyway she added me, she was now a Facebook friend
So I messaged her, "You're the cutest girl I've ever seen
I want to suck your nipples hard
And I want to flick your bean
Oh and I want to lick your arsehole!"
She was like "Are you for real?"

But after a few more messages like the one above
She agreed to go out with me for a meal
Happy days I thought to myself
She was prepared to drive to Whitstable and stay over
Whitstable is quite a lengthy drive
If you're setting off from Dover
Now I've got to admit I was excited
She looked pretty fit the day I'd met her
I'd checked out all her Facebook pics
In which she looked just as good or better
I'd booked a table in an expensive restaurant
I was prepared to spend a lot of money
I mean as far as I was aware
This was one fucking sexy single mummy
But things aren't always as they seem
Some things can cause confusion
She'd had a baggy hoody on when I met her
Which created an optical illusion
See I just assumed that inside that hoody
Was a half decent little figure
But when she got out of her car
I didn't jump for joy like Tigger
See now there was no hoody
She had dressed up in a dress
But she looked like a fucking skeleton
And if I had to take a guess
I'd say this girl was undernourished
She was nowt but skin and bone
Her ribs stuck out so fucking much
She looked like a xylophone
Plus she'd had her hair cut
It had been shoulder length at least
Now this skinny bitch had hair
Like a badly trimmed wildebeest
How can I put this?
She looked like an abandoned R.S.P.C.A. chiwawa
And I had to take it to the restaurant
In just under half an hour

But being the consummate professional
I didn't let on that I was in a state of shock
Somewhere between the skin and bone
Would be some sort of hole to stick my cock
So I walked with her to the restaurant
She was nervous, shy and twitchy
I squeezed her butt but it was boney
I squeezed her tit and it was titchy
Anyway we sat down at the table
But to her the menu may has well have been in Japanese
She looked at it then started twitching
Fuck! I thought, this fucked up chiwawa must have fleas
"I've never been anywhere as posh as this!"
Said the blonde haired chiwawa
With that the waiter brought the wine
At which point my scrawny date began to cower
However not being the kinda guy
To let a situation get on top of me
I said "Listen if you're gonna barf up your meal
Just order a starter for your tea
Cos the main meals here are pricey
So if you're bulimic it's ok
Just don't go ordering the lobster
Cos it's me that's gotta pay!!"
"I'm not a bulimic!" she answered
"I'm just on a really extreme diet!"
At least I'd broken the ice
Up until now the twitchy fuck had been dead quiet!
"I only eat porridge that's all I eat
It's helped me lose a ton of weight!!"
"Ok Goldilocks, well well done you
Your porridge diet has worked great!!"
I then called over the nearest waiter
And ordered my choice of food
Goldilocks still had no clue what to get
So I told the waiter dude
"And she would like to order
Two carrot sticks and one small tiny piece of bread!"

If looks could kill I'm in no doubt
Her look would have killed me stone cold dead
She decided to order the same as me
And to be fair she did quite well
She ate at least half of her meal
Which for her must have been like living hell!
We'd done two bottles of wine by now
She was now more chatty and less shy
She admitted she had been really nervous
But was now ok cos I was such an easy going guy
Then she got up and went to the toilet
She was in there quite a while
"You just threw up that meal didn't you?"
I said upon her return with an enigmatic smile
"Just admit it you dirty porridge thief!"
I said in the voice of Big Daddy Bear
"No I promise I didn't I know that's what it looks like
But I didn't I promise I swear!!"
We left the restaurant shortly after
And went to a wine bar for more wine
By this point we'd kissed
And were getting on fine
We went back to my house
Goldilocks got into my bed
I started licking her pussy
But then a thought entered my head
I thought 'I can feel a fart coming on
And it could be a whopper
To fart in this situation
Well it just wouldn't be proper'
So I stopped licking her minge
Left my bedroom and stepped on to my landing
Shut the door, did my fart
But what I weren't understanding
Was how my big fart
Became a big shit
My new white Calvin Klien pants
Had suddenly become weighed down quite a bit

I stood there on my landing
With a big brick of shit in my pants
Sexy huh? Ok I admit it
This isn't one of my sexier rants!
I waddled down the stairs
Like I was in a three legged race
I knew this was bad
But I had a silly grin on my face
I waddled into the bathroom
Then flipped the shit into the bog
This weren't no small curler
This was a big shitty log
I took my pants off
Then stuck them in the washing machine
They had the biggest skid mark in them
You would ever have seen
I got some pants from the laundry basket
And put those on instead
Then walked back up my stairs
And got back into bed
I carried on licking Goldilocks minge
Like nothing untoward had gone down
She had no idea that my C.K. pants
Which had been white were now brown
But with that shit done and dusted
I could now get down to some fucking
I stuck my thumb up her bum
Whilst my cock she was sucking
Her pussy was quite hollow
And bizarrely so was the inside of her arse
And this next bit of my story
Well it may come across as somewhat of a farce
See I started to fuck her
She made me strap up fair enough
I was happy to have some protection
From this ropey Dover hoes muff
But it didn't feel great if I'm honest
Plus I was upset that she didn't turn out to be fitter

So I pulled my cock out of her cunt
And whapped it straight up her shitter
I fucked her for a while
But I still couldn't cum
Her fanny was spacious
But unpredictably so was her bum!
I blamed it on the condom
It's all the Jonny's fault there's no doubt
"Ok" she said "Take it off but remember
That you have to pull out!"
The sex continued sporadically
Both holes I kept hitting
I'd put to the back of my mind
The dirty Calvin Klien pants and the shitting
But I needed to spunk now
I was so close to cumming
Perhaps I could ejaculate
If I gave her one last ruthless bumming
And as I bummed her into submission
I finally came
Inside her arse or was it?
See both holes felt the same
I could have sworn it was her anus
That I'd just been protruding
But it was in fact her pussy
How fucking eluding!
She was like "I told you to pull out
Now I've got to get the morning after pill thanks a lot
Don't tell me you didn't remember
Don't say you forgot!!"
"Oh I didn't forget
I just thought I was fucking your pooper!"
"You thought my fanny was my arse?"
"Why yes isn't that super
Cos that means your fanny must be tight
For me to think that!!"
I didn't tell her the inside of her arse
Felt as fucking hollow as the inside of her twat

Darnel sanchez

That they were both equally as hollow and empty
Like two great big giant caves
Two perfect venues for ravers to go
To hold big illegal raves
I mean how can it be
That a girl who's just bone and skin
Has an arsehole so spacious
It could fit rave monkeys in?
She was basically a skeleton
With nothing in the middle
How the fuck she's alive
Is one gigantic riddle!
Yeah Goldilocks weren't happy
When she left the next day
But she did take the morning after pill
Much to my relief I'm thankful to say
And just like the story of Goldilocks
There is a moral to this story too
So pay attention to this bit
If it's the last thing that you do!
Remember in Goldilocks and the Three Bears
The bears were robbed so get a pad and pen and take notes
Do not trust Goldilocks she's still a porridge thief
She snuck out of my house in the morning
Full of my hot oats!!!

Big Fuzzy in Little China

I'd woken up feeling horny
So I booked myself a morning whore
It's just way too fucking easy
When there's a brothel practically next door
I had a bath, smoked a J, did a Viagra
Then went off to see
If this week's Chinese offering
Was a ten out of ten or just a three
To my delight this one was a cracker
Really really sexy about a nine
Lovely face, amazing tits
This whore was fucking fine
I even licked her pussy
Didn't even care that she was a hooker
I just pretended I was her first punter
The only guy to ever book her!
Her pussy was amazing and yes I came
Far too quick which was annoying
Cos fucking this particular Chinese whore
Was something I was seriously enjoying
But rules are rules and you only get to cum once
Then you can have a massage in what's left of your time
And within ten minutes I'd shot my bolt
And filled my Johnny full of slime
But as I lay there getting massaged
I thought you know what I might come back
£120 a day on sex is quite a lot
But I really wanted another crack
At fucking this Chinese stunner
So during the course of the next 8 hours
I drank some wine, smoked some weed, did half an E
Took another Viagra and increased my super powers!
I phoned up and booked her a second time
Went back over at half past ten

The hooker opened the door, she was naked
I was like "Hi me again!!"
Only this time I had the magic wand
I wanted to go all out on this hoe
"What is that?" she asked me
"It's my massager wand please feel free to have a go!"
So she started to play with the massager
Trying to massage my back but I said "Ok enough!"
Then I took it back, laid her down
And began to use it on her muff
Now considering this girl was a prozzie
We had amazing chemistry
We fucked for much longer than my 30 minutes
As she was proper kissing me
Now that's normally a no no
Whores don't normally passionately kiss with tongues
Hers was so far down my throat
It was tickling my lunges
Now you can say that prostitution isn't right
But in this case that statements just berserk
This girl was enjoying fucking me
She was really fucking happy in her work
Too happy actually cos after an hour
Of the bed squeaking and her loud vocals
The Chinese man who owned the house
Was shouting "Shu'up or you'll wake the locals!!"
So we took it down a notch or two
But her cunt I still kept my cock in
Until the Chinese triad pimp
Started shouting in Chinese and knocking
On the wall of the bedroom
The whore said "Ok he's got mad
Your time was up 45 minutes ago!!"
"I guess that's my fault, I'm sorry, my bad!!"
I still hadn't got my happy ending
I hadn't actually cum
Not that that really bothered me
In no way was I glum

Darnel sanchez

I'd already had one happy ending
In the morning, earlier on that day
And this was the best Chinese whore
I'd ever encountered I think I'd have to say
She was genuinely sorry that I had to go
And people say romance is dead
Admit it, this poem right here
Is probably the most romantic thing you've ever read!!

Cheryl Cole

In the Chinese brothel
In the bedroom
Is a giant poster of Cheryl Cole!
So you can stare at sexy Cheryl
Whilst a Chinese brass
Polishes your pole
Yes I know I shouldn't be in brothels
It's not right
And I'm not proud
But at least whilst I'm banging whores
I'm actually thinking of
One of the sluts from Girls Aloud!!

Who's Been Eating My Arsehole?

I kept on texting Goldilocks
Yeah ok she was too skinny
But if I'd mugged her off completely
I'd have been a stupid ninny
Cos she was happy to let me bum her
And from 9 am-3 pm her son would be at school
Which meant if I was working over her way
And kept things between us cool
Then she'd be ok with me poppin in for a bit
A bit of poo hole intrusion
So over the course of the next few months
I maintained the illusion
That I really liked her
Nice things to her I would often say
So she was relatively happy
With me spontaneously turning up during the day
It was a wee bit awkward though
Cos I'd be sober and my lust for her was fake
She'd be all edgy, so would I, but despite that
I'd still without fail fucking make
Her suck my penis until it was hard
Then I'd stick it straight up her bony butt
And sodimise her ruthlessly
Until I bust a nut!
Then once I'd filled her shit pit
To the point of overflowing
I'd get dressed give her a kiss
And say "I'd better get a going
Gotta get some surveys
Gotta go and do my thing!!"
She'd stand there looking a bit despondent
As my jizz leaked out her ring!
But I stopped seeing her around the time
That head office stopped sending me to work in Dover

Our anal romance fizzled out
It had been fun but it was over!
No more bumming Goldilocks
I let the poor girl be
She had enough on her plate
Without getting repeatedly bummed by me
Actually in no way did she have enough on her plate
She clearly could've done with a whole lot more
That girl needed feeding up
She looked like a fucking prisoner of war!
Ha! Enough on her plate! I promise you
There really was no pun intended
Anyway like I said, I stopped seeing Goldilocks
Which is why this rhyme about her's ended!!!

Nose Rope

When I was a little lad
Some really weird stuff came out my nose
It was like some kinda intertwined rope
The length of a garden hose
I'm not talking about an elongated bogie
Or a big ol' line of snot
I'm talking actual proper rope
And to this day I've still not
Found anyone else that this has happened to
Why was I born with rope inside my head
I'd pull and pull and pull at it
But the moment I would dread
Was the moment when I'd feel a tug
Like it was somehow attached to my brain
For it was at this point of pulling
That anymore pulling caused me pain
Which meant it must be time to snap it
I'd snap the rope, the pain would stop
Then all the nose rope that I'd pulled out
Would fall yes it would drop
Into the sink that I'd leant over
This ordeal happened about five times I guess
Back then I thought it must be normal
But now I think that much much less
What was it? Was it a brain restraint?
Some ropey alien parasite? What do you think?
What the fuck was all the weird woven string
That I'd pull out then snap off into the sink?
Was it my emergency cord?
Please pull if you're in trouble!
I'd pull it but all that happened as a result
Was that the length of the rope would double!
It's still an unsolved mystery
I've looked online but there's nowt about it

Perhaps I should consult a nose specialist
Would they nose? Who nose? I doubt it
So if you have any information
About ropey nasal string
Please Facebook me or text me
Tweet me, give me a ring
Because I'd love to solve this riddle
So if you can help me please be kind
And explain to me the purpose of the nose rope
And why I have a ball of string inside my mind!!!

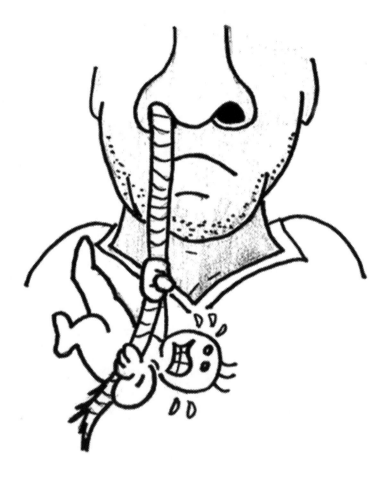

Why Don't You Drive?

"Why don't you drive?"
People often enquire
"Well for one
I don't ever want to change a car tyre!"
"Also I don't want to run animals over
Or crash!
Plus cars cost
Shit loads of cash!
They deplete in value
Quicker than a Fifa video game
And I can say for certain
No one will ever be able to blame
Me for causing an accident on the roads
In fact if I drove I doubt you'd still be alive
I would've driven whilst intoxicated and killed you
But relax I won't ever drink drive
Cos I won't be driving a motor
You won't see me in the fast lane
Cos I'll be on the top deck of a bus
Or sat in first class on a train!!!!

Take A Walk On The Wild Side

I've never had a girl date me for my car
She wouldn't have got driven very far
I've never been a glorified taxi cab for a hoe
"Give me a lift" I don't drive bitch
I'll walk you there, where would you like to go???

I Caught Cabs!

I never caught syphilis
I never caught crabs
But cos I've never had a car
I've caught a lot of cabs!!

Pandemic

Pandas are almost extinct
Extinct like Christopher Reeves
The male panda is my super hero
Put him with a girl panda
And he eats, shoots and leaves!!!

Pandamonium

I love pandas
They are my second favourite animal of all time
They are black and white and Asian
Thus this is not a racist rhyme!!

Panda To My Demands

I had fourteen soft toy pandas as a kid
But I had no damn bamboo
I made a hole in the biggest ones bum
So it's stuffing it would poo
Sometimes I liked to rape it
I would take it by surprise
One time it struggled so I punched it twice
And gave it two black eyes!!

The Gurney Journey

Let me take you on a journey
My journey home from work from Mobiles 4U
It was the year two thousand
I was a coke fiend! "Achoo!"
Just sneezed out half a gram
Cocaine bogies sure I kept um
I was sniffin so much bugle
I'm surprised I have a septum!
Ok let's start this journey
A train journey from Hastings (Sussex East)
A long journey back to Margate
So I'd packed myself a feast
Of weed, cocaine and alcohol
To make my journey a little easier to bare
A two hour journey on a two cart train
No train ticket, no train fare!
Now back in the year two thousand
Trains were right old smelly buggers
No cameras, separate compartments
Perfect environment for muggers
But you also had a lot of privacy
If you were in a compartment the curtains you could close
On this particular journey I was in a compartment
Shovelling cocaine up my nose!
I had lines racked up on the drinks shelf
Four cans of Stella and a lit joint
I needed a piss, was gonna go find a toilet
But then thought what's the point
I'd piss in my compartment
"Piss piss piss" that pissing was me
Then the door of my compartment opened
And I turned around to see
The ticket man oh dear
What a sight for sore eyes

Lines racked up, lit joint in my mouth
Beer in hand, pissing "Surprise!"
"Have you got a ticket sir?
On second thoughts never mind!!"
Me, pissing in the corner
He clearly did not expect to find
Amazingly he left me to it
I must have looked proper nutty
"Look away or I'll shank you bruv
Cutty cutty cutty!"
Yeah if I'd been that ticket man
I'd have fucked off too!
Ok back to my journey
You still with me? Yes you!!
Good! Eventually I got home
Back to Jane my missus
Her parents had Marie that night
Jane was happy to see me and bombarded me with kisses
Amazingly we were getting on and we'd been invited
To Jodie's birthday do at a pub 'The Three Legged Toad'
I'd only just got back from work
I was off my nut already and it showed
No time to rest my journey wasn't over
Had to leave with Jane and head to Jodie's party
I looked suave and debonair
Jane looked cheap and tarty
When we arrived I found my mate Wills
He gave me two big E's
"Dazzy son you look fucked already
You'll look more fucked after these!"
I double dropped the ecstasy
Not the smartest idea
It curdled with the cocaine
The weed and the cans of beer
Within about half an hour
I was all over the fucking show
I was seeing four of everything
I was more fucked than you could know

Darnel sanchez

This was back when you could smoke in pubs
And as I puffed on a fag
The smoke went down the wrong way
I regretted taking that last drag
I vomited in my mouth
I held it in and ran
Get out the pub without throwing up
Was my fucking plan
Puke was squirting out the sides of my mouth
As I ran out the door
"Blugghh blaaughhh bluagghh"
I couldn't hold it anymore
I was throwing up outside the pub
Jane came out to see my grand display
"Oh my God he's gonna die!"
Was all the crazy bitch could say
To be fair I was pretty fucked
My eyes apparently had rolled back
I couldn't focus on very much
All I could do was yack
Wills came out and talked to me
He asked if I was compos mentis
I was fine inside my own head
But I was throwing up the day befores Frey Bentos
I was proper cunted
So Jane got Wills to take us back
This was the first night in ages me and Jane had gone out together
And I almost gave her a heart attack
She really thought I was gonna snuff it
She'd never seen me so close to death
I looked like a fucking meth head
Ten years before anyone had invented meth
Anyway we went home and watched a film
'The Bone Collector' I watched it in 3D
This was before the days of 3D televisions
Yet somehow my tv picture improved on E!
And that was the end of my journey
Me sat on my sofa gurning

I hope you all enjoyed the journey
And hopefully along the way you've all been learning
A little bit about how badly behaved I was
How I liked to live life to excess
And how a simple journey back from work
Could end up with me being a fucking drugged up mess!!

Wheezy Does It!

Sign up to plentyoffish.com
That's what my pals kept saying
It's free and there's loads of hoes on there
That right now you could be laying!
So I set up a P.O.F. account
And began to search for fish
I chatted to a bunch of hoes
Who were ok or ok'ish
But one hoe that I messaged
Seemed to be a winner
So usual drill I asked her out
For drinks or maybe dinner!
This hoe lived quite near to me
In Herne Bay to be precise
She had a half decent face
Yep this hoe seemed rather nice
Turned out she was an actress
Not full time just every now and then
She'd been on tv once or twice
And was hoping to appear on tv again
But for now she was rehearsing for a play
In a theatre not far from my home address
So she suggested after her rehearsal we meet up
Obviously I answered 'Yes'
I met her outside the theatre
At around about half past nine
We went to my favourite wine bar
Where we sat and drank some wine
We got on rather well I'd say
In fact it was her that I think suggested
That the bag of weed that she'd just bought
Should be took back to my house and tested
So we snuggled up on my sofa
And smoked a joint or two

She asked if she could stay the night
As I rubbed her actress foo
Obviously I said that she could stay
I was stoned and I was happy
We were having a romantic evening
Until rudely interrupted by my mate Dappy
Yes at about midnight my door burst open
It was Dappy and doorman Dan
Trying to get me down the Brewery Bar
At least I think that was their plan
But I had to disappoint them
Shame I'm sure had I gone it'd have been quite good
Seeing as how I'd have got the chance to hang out
With D.J. Timothy Westwood!
But I turned them down
So off they went
My romantic evening in
I didn't let them dent!
Not long after they left we went up to bed!
But when this girl took off her tights
A load of extra fat appeared
Guess this was gonna just be one of those nights
I mean I knew she was a bit squishy
But how did I manage to miss
All her hidden blubber
Didn't dream she was as fat as this
Never mind I'd fucked fat girls before
One more fatty wouldn't fucking matter
But with each item of clothing she took off
She got another two stone fatter
The big fat useless squishy hump
Said she didn't really like sex that much
But I was not deterred
And stuck my face right in her crutch!
Her cunt weren't in good nic at all
She'd not done her pelvic thrusts I'm guessing
And I still couldn't believe that she had gained
About 8 stone simply by undressing!

Anyway I stuck my throbbing penis
Into her big slimy rubbish moo'ey
Fucking disgusting thing it was
All big and wet and gooey!
No this was no good at all
Time to introduce the clit massager
Perhaps it would cause her pussy to tense up
Shame my cocks not four times larger
But it's not so out came my trusted sex toy
And I used the same blag I'd used before
The same blag I used with Troll Face, Kay Why,
Tufts, Slaps, Goldilocks and at least one Chinese whore
"This is my back massager for my back
But I want to try it on your minge"
This was about to be its eighth recipient
Oops did that make you cringe?
I put it on to full power
And made her hold it on her clit
"Ooww ahh oohh mmm ah ooshh
Jesus fuck damn holy shit!"
Yeah she loved the power of the magic wand
It sure did hit the spot
I certainly made a good call buying that thing
I mean it's come into play a lot
Ok so there I was banging this fatty
Whilst she held the wand between her flaps
(Only two or three months previous to this
It had been between the legs of Mistress Slaps)
Thing is I couldn't fucking cum
Cumming with this fat fuck weren't fucking easy
Then she had an asthma attack
And became really really wheezy
I tried to keep on fucking her
As she tried desperately to find her huffa
Her shit cunt and surprise fat had pissed me off
But I cheered up watching her suffer
She reached down and found her asthma pump
And after taking one last giant puff

Said "I don't think I can carry on
I think I've had enough
For fucks sake! I still hadn't spunked
And it weren't for lack of trying
Annoyingly I'd almost cum
Cos her fanny had tightened up whilst she was dying!
But I went to sleep and let her rest
Then in the morning I tried again
I fucked her and fucked her
I was sure I'd cum eventually I just didn't know when
I really wasn't enjoying the sex
With this big fat fucking joker
I could poke her and poke her
And poke her and poke her
But I weren't gonna ejaculate
I just weren't gonna cum
Woulda probably had more success
If I'd been fucking honey boo boo's fat mum!
So I made a tough judgement call
And told Wheezy I was gonna go make coffee and toast
And nip to the post office
To post some important post
But what I actually did
When I went down to my kitchen
Was phone up the Chinese brothel
To see if they had a new Chinese bitch in
"Yes you come now sir
New girl she'll be waiting for you!"
"Cool that's perfect
That's just what I'll do!"
So I left the toast in the toaster
And walked out my front door
Over the road around the corner
To the brothel to go see the whore
I was ready to cum
My balls were about to explode
I had to cum badly
And to be fair it probably showed

The Chinese whore was a cracker
Good looking, small and petite
I bent her over and fucked her
Pulled out, took the Johnny off and spunked on her feet
I'd paid for half an hour
But was done in ten minutes or so
Easy mornings fucking money
For this particular Chinese fucking hoe
Anyway I skipped back to my house
Made the coffee and toast and went back to bed
"So are you planning on fucking me all day?"
The fat wheezy bird said
"Naah I think I'll just have a cuddle
I don't feel like sex anymore!"
Little did she know I'd just spunked
All over the feet of a fit Chinese whore!!!

Gaybrahams Ex!

Back when I was still at school
There was this one kid named Gaybraham
The bentest ginger kid you could hope to meet
Am I too harsh? Perhaps I am!
Anyway I found Gaybraham annoying
He was such a ginger fagg
So you can imagine my frustration
When he pulled a younger looking slag
Who he then started fucking dating
Surely this romance was a sham
I mean what the fuck did this sexy slut
See in a ginger poof like Gaybraham?
Now admittedly this was a long time ago
Seriously to be fair I mean
This was in the last year of school
I was still only fifteen
But it really fucking bugged me
This bird back then was tidy
Gaybraham was as bent as a two bob note
He was ginger, queer and snidey
So when I spotted his ex from all those years ago
On Plenty of Fish one day
I messaged her saying "I know you
You went out with Gaybraham the gay"
"Hello yes I remember you
How the devil are you doing?"
"I'm fine, you look good"
Thinking this is someone I one day need to write about me screwin
Because if I'm being honest
She didn't look good, she weren't sexy anymore
Time had taken its toll
She weren't a teenager now she was thirty four!
Plus she had two children
And she'd clearly put on weight

But what the hell, I'd wanted to fuck her all those years ago
So to fuck her now would still be great!
Anyway I got her to come to Whitstable
I took her to my favourite wine bar for drinks
She really didn't look that sexy
But she'd be cheaper than those rental chinks
So I listened intently to her bollocks
About her two boys and how they were so cute and clever
How one liked to dress up like a soldier
Yeah, ok, great, superb, whatever
"Blah blah blah my son this
Blah blah blah my son that"
This was one tedious hoe
That really did deserve a scoop and splat!
We ended up back at my house
I smoked a joint and then I took her
Up to my bedroom, lights off
As I mentioned before she weren't much of a looker!
But I had to do this for old times sake
My way of rectifying her error from the past
The fact she dated Gaybraham instead of me
Well a dark shadow on my life that fucking cast
So I got her fanny out for inspection
Her cunt was in quite good nick
So I pulled down my underpants
And into her mouth I shoved my dick
Strangely she looked slimmer naked
Than she did with her clothes on
And I was bizarrely happy to be sticking my cock
In the same pussy that Gaybraham's had once gone
Her cunt felt just right inside
And her tits were big and round
"What's this thing?" she asked inquisitively
"This thing on the ground?"
"Oh it's my back massager for my bad back
Hold on look I'll show!"
"You sure it's for your bad back?
You forget I know people that know you!"

"Honestly it is a back massager
Although I suppose it would work on a clit!"
At which point I turned it on to full power
Then massaged her pussy with it for a bit!
In the darkness I did enjoy the sex
I imagined her as she was all those years before
When she was dating Gaybraham
Back when she was a little teenage whore
And with that image fixed in my mind
I withdrew and out shot my manfat
On to her tummy which I then scooped up
And wiped into her face 'kasplat'
But in the morning in the daylight
Well the fantasy was destroyed
She went back to being the type of single mum
I normally try my hardest to avoid
I made it clear I wasn't interested in anything more
Than that one night of loveless sex
I then told her the only reason she even got that
Was literally only because Gaybraham was her ex!!

Shakey Hair

Bloody hell I'm going bald
But unfortunately I can't afford
Hair implants like Wayne Rooney
My scalp looks like it's pulling a moony
I'm still young it's just not fair
That's why I use magic shakey hair!!

Gas

In gas and electric door knocking
Legends were created
But by the general public
Our kind were fucking hated
Blaggers, liars, pushy buggers
Imposing, misleading, doorstep muggers!
I was banned from the industry three times
For my dodgy doorstep crimes
Well now everyone's been banned from doing it
Cos of years and years of dodgy shit!!

The Big Fuzzy House

I'd come to the conclusion that I was missing Slaps
She was almost my perfect match
Chris on the other hand
Was happy with his latest bit of snatch
Which was doing my fucking nut in
I'm afraid I have to say
I was happy Chris was happy
His whole demeanour got more gay
But his girlfriend Mumpy was a teacher
And teachers make me feel uneasy
I couldn't help but think that Chris's bird
Found me immoral, crass and sleazy
Which is fine but in my own house
I don't like to feel like I'm being judged
And I didn't like the noises that she made
Whilst fucking Chris up until he sludged
Once he'd cum it would all go quiet
But then he'd have another crack
A few weeks previous he was moaning about Slaps making noise
And this role reversal was just plain whack
I was comfort eating take aways
And having fry ups every day
And drinking loads and smoking loads
To make the pissed off feeling go away
But this unhealthy life style
Began to take its toll
I was now a lot more fatter
Than back when I was fucking Troll Face the troll
Plus I'd started getting pains in my kidney
And pains in my chest
This made me a little paranoid
And had me feeling stressed

I really thought my time was almost up
And that made me start to worry
I didn't want to die without doing a second book
But if I were to do that I'd have to hurry
Time was not on my side
I felt the Grim Reaper on my shoulder
Death please wait until
I'm at least a few years older
But I weren't convinced that death was listening
I had to act fast no time to wait
I had to write a second book
Before it was too late
So I began writing Fifty Feels Of Fuzz
The Autorhymeography Part Two
I had a lot of shit to say
And I had a lot of work to do
I no longer cared about bitches
Or anything else for that matter
I was in full blown author mode
Book crazy, mad as a hatter
See to write an autobiography in rhyme
Is no walk in the park
Especially when the content you are tackling
Is so painful, deep and dark
I started eating healthy
Vegetables, fruit and bran
Desperately trying to buy more time
To execute my plan
My plan of unleashing my pent up fury
About the D.N.A. test and baby 'It'
I wanted to write about Fudgey, Troll Face,
The Chinese whores, lizard people and some other shit
So I spent every possible minute
Writing rhymes for the book, you see I had to
I didn't go out and socialise
I stayed in and I was glad to

Before I knew it Christmas was upon me
I took time out to buy everyone a present
I tried really hard to buy my family special things
That might make their Christmas Day more pleasant!
I spent Christmas with my mother
We had a nice day I love my mum
I feel sorry for people with no family
Their December 25th must be glum!
But see whilst everyone else at Christmas
Pigs out and drinks too much
I did the fucking opposite
Cos I do things double dutch
I had been drinking too much and over eating
All year fucking long
Then Christmas came and it dawned on me
Where I'd been going wrong
Maybe my life of excess
Should be confined to a few weeks of the year
Maybe I should drink fruit juice when I get home
Instead of cans of beer
All this over eating is not good
I should really join a gym
David Hay, he looks ok
I want to look like him
Turn all my flubber into muscle
Maybe get bang on it, do some roids
I could get ripped, become a doorman
And beat up teenage mongaloids!
Anyway back to the story
Spending Christmas with my mother
New Year's Eve, well New Year's Eve
Was unlike any other
In that I let all my friends down
I blew them out and I stayed in
I didn't feel like drinking any alcohol
No rum, no port, no gin

Darnel sanchez

I just stayed in with mum and had a Horlicks
Instead of going out and licking whores
This was the first New Year's Eve in centuries
I'd not been out bustin moves on pub or club dance floors
So yeah that was my Christmas and my New Years
Twenty twelve slash twenty thirteen
I was feeling like a washed up, burnt out
On the verge of death has been!!

Wembley David Icke

Fudgey had bought tickets
Almost a year ago
We'd split up soon after
Then Troll Face was my hoe
That didn't last long either
But then Slaps came along
"Slaps do you fancy seeing David Icke?"
I asked as I pulled off her neon thong
"Sure I'll come see him with you
If you'd like me there!"
"Yes I'd like you to accompany me!"
I replied whilst removing Slaps bright pink underwear
Only Slaps and I broke up
So I still had a spare ticket
I asked her if she'd still like to go
And she told me where to stick it!
I was gonna ask my mother
I'd gotten her into David Icke
But Jane actually suggested Marie
Would most probably quite like
To go with me to Wembley
So I asked Marie to come
She'd been schooled on all things lizard
My daughter isn't dumb
She knows the way the world works
She knows what's wrong and what is right
She realises it's the reptoid elites
That are responsible for the humans plight
She was happy to keep me company
Even though it was going to be a long 12 hour talk
Most kids her age in Thanet are so backward

They're still watching Charlie Chalk
But not my little Moof Bear
She's not an inbred Mong
12 hours is quite a while to have to sit
It is a tad bit long
But for the most part Marie stayed focused
Most of the info she absorbed and understood
Say what you like about David Icke
When it comes to talking unscripted he's fucking good!
I'm not gonna rhyme in depth about what he covered
Are you kidding that would be a book in itself
Instead I'll summarise the bullet points
Which were: the systematic thiefdom of peoples wealth,
The Rockefellas, the Rothchilds, corporate greed,
Subliminal messages and images, the agenda, the elite,
The Illuminati, our reality being beamed from Saturn,
Left brain, right brain, the shit in what we eat,
Negative emotions creating negative energy
Counteracting that by being compassionate and kind
Why they want World War 3, 911, the Middle East,
The Freemasons, micro chipping, having an open mind,
Manipulation of the masses, problem, reaction, solution
Love being the ultimate answer, war being bad
Ancient civilisations, the Mayans, pyramids
The moon being hollow, the world's gone mad
The destruction of the rainforest, G.M.O.'s
Sheeple, politicians, the truth about Bin Laden
Fluoride in water, chemtrails, Israel,
Why it's best to grow your own food in your garden
Interdimensional energy vampires, Palestine,
The N.W.O, child sacrifices, peado rings,
Charles and Savile being friends, Bohemain Grove,
The Bilderberg Group, plus some other things!
For twenty five years the Ickesta
Has been researching, he the man

Darnel sanchez

And over the years he has exposed
And picked apart the Illuminastys plan
I'm 90% behind him, I almost trust him
But I'm no longer 100% sure
I was at one stage I really was
But I'm not that certain anymore!
I'll explain why a bit later
For now I'll give the Ickesta his due
He was captivating live at Wembley
Even if only half what he said was true!!

Gareth Icke

I'm friends with David Ickes son Gareth
Well I'm friends with him on Facebook at least
He shares the same views that his Dad has
About the Royals, the nature of reality, the Middle East!
He fascinates me if I'm honest
I mean what must it be like having a dad like Ghandi
Gareth is one chap I'd love to have a chat with
In a pub over a shandy!
But yeah Gareth Icke is a musician
A singer, he's actually pretty good
And on the missing Wogan Show I figured he could shed some light
I mean if anyone could he could
So I hit him with it one day
Told him all about my sighting
Told him that I'd wrote about it in my rhyme
Cos that's how I do my writing!
He admitted it was weird
But never addressed the issue again
That issue being that the only Wogan interview
Left on the net was the 2nd one called 'Now and Then'
The mystery of the freaky lizard dude
And the vanishing Wogan Show
Is a mystery that looks set to stay a mystery
An answer to why it disappeared no one seems to know!
Anyway obviously Gareth didn't want to talk about it
So I thought I better not keep prying
I'd put up a £500 reward in Fifty Feels of Fuzz
And I know some people were really trying
To find the studio audience footage from that show
But as of yet no one's succeeded
I was hoping someone would've found it

Cos that £500 they really needed
I guess something's are best left unfound
I've pissed off the reptoids of that I'm certain
I don't want to piss them off too much though
So on this case I think I'll close the curtain!
Anyway Gareth Icke I chat to on Facebook
About football and non-lizard stuff
He seems like a decent human being
And as a kid I'm sure he had it rough
What with David Icke being his dad
I expect he had to deal with loads of shit
So I figured I'd send him Fifty Feels of Fuzz
To cheer him up a bit
I said "Yo G do you want a free copy
Of Fifty Feels of Fuzz my new book?"
"Sure I'd love one!" so I sent him one
His address in Derby by now I'd took
So yeah I sent him Fifty Feels of Fuzz
He told me he'd received it
David Ickes son Gareth has my book
I myself can barely believe it
Although he's never told me he enjoyed it
He might not have even read it
Or he found it fucking offensive
Although if he had then to me he would have said it
I know he's against prostitution
And in Fifty Feels there's whores galore
But it sounds so much worse than it is
I've never slept with a mistreated whore
The ones I've fucked have been escorts
There's been no nasty pimp and I'm in no doubt
That these girls do it of their own free will
Cos they need money and all I do is help them out
Anyway Gareth Icke is still my Facebook friend

And I'm still a fan of him and his dad
Jonathan Ross has my first book
Gareth Icke has my second and I'm glad
That people in the public eye
Own books full of my amazing rhyme
But which celebrity will get this one?
Who's turn will it be this time?
I'm thinking maybe Ben Elton
Or Public Enemy's Professor Griff
I'll have a proper think about it
Once I'm done smoking this spliff!!!

Buzz Right Ear!

Just the other side of the railway embankment
Across from my mums house there was a school
And sometimes in the summertime
When no kids were there at all
I would hear this high pitched frequency
It really hurt my ears and gave me a headache
I'd try to cover my ears
But little difference did it make
It seemed like it was coming from
The school recreation ground
It really was a horrible high pitched
Sonic wave type sound!
The thing that really puzzled me
Was that my mum and dad could not hear it
Why the fuck was I the only one
They were just as fucking near it
Sometimes it would stop as if it'd been switched off
Then it would come back even worse
Now looking back on it I'm almost certain they were trialling
The sonic blast machine that the government now uses to disperse
Gangs of youths away from problem areas
See it only works on teenage girls and boys
Somehow adults are unaffected
They are in no way able to hear the noise
Sounds pretty fucking cunty and a bit far fetched
Well it's real just look it up on Wikipedia
It was even mentioned some years ago
On mainstream fucking media
And I'm sure now I was caught up in its testing
Fucking government Nazi scum
You were the reason why during the school holidays

My ears would sometimes hear a high pitched hum
Just shows you the type of horrible shit
The government likes to do
Well guess what you government fucks
I'm gonna invent a sonic frequency
That only works on government pricks like you!!

Maccy D's

I'm three years clean of Maccy D's
I don't want dia-b-e-tees!
Jamie Oliver I dissed you in book two
But I've squashed that beef I respect you
You took McDonalds to court and you won
Cos of the toxic crap they stick in a bun!!

Quim

There was this girl on Facebook
From Canterbury named Quim
Not the prettiest of girls
And more visits to the gym
Would have done her the world of good
Anyway for about a year or so
I kept arranging to meet up with
This chunky below average looking hoe
But time and time and time again
Yes time after time after time
I'd end up mugging off this hoe
Cos birds like her are a dozen a dime
You know, kinda fat, had a kid
Had a face that looked all dumpy
I couldn't be arsed to meet up with her
Just on the off chance of rumpy pumpy
I didn't want to take her out in public
Cos I'm a shallow nasty git
If I'm taking a girl out on a date
Then she's gotta look semi fit
But I was going through a crisis
During early two thousand thirteen
Events leading up to this point
Had made me ruthless, cold and mean
I'd used plenty of fucking fish.com
But not to find the love of my life
I weren't searching for a girlfriend,
Or a companion or wife
I'd used it to take advantage
Of desperate vulnerable single women
And one time when I scrolled through its offerings
I found the local hoe list had this fat quim in
"Hello Quim fancy you being on here!"
I messaged just for fun

"I think we should finally get together
It's a good idea ain't it hun?"
See my standards had took a nose dive
Just look at Gaybrahams ex and Wheezy
I should have been banging fitter birds
Like my ex Fudgey's sister Cheesy
But I'd decided to just fuck anything
Any pussy is better than none
At least fat birds are fucking grateful
And no matter what you do to them they won't run
So after two years of mugging off
This fat hoe Quim I then decided
To actually go out for drinks with her
Cos a cunt to fucking fuck she clearly provided
Anyway it was January, it was snowing
The snow lay even, deep and crisp
When I saw Quim in the pub
She looked like the fat fairy from Willow the Wisp
Actually much fatter that I'd anticipated
Much larger than I thought she'd be
So I figured I'd confine our date to the back of the pub
Where less people were likely to see
I drank about five pints of Stella
Enough to get my beer goggles on
Whatever standards I'd had in the past
Were now well long fucking gone!
She wanted to go to a club
But I weren't really happy with that
I said "I think we should just buy a bottle of wine
And head back to your flat!"
A point I think now I should really mention
Is the fact all night I had with me a J.D. sports bag
Which contained my trusty fanny massager
And some Viagra's, essential things for fucking this slag
So yeah we got back to her flat
I passionately kissed her
I wondered if this was another slack fannied slut
That might want me to fist her!

We went to her bedroom
I laid the fat cunt down on her bed
I took off her panties they were big
Like a tent if tents were lacy and red!
Ahh another big sweaty fanny
Big sweaty fannies are shit
So I pulled the massager out
And said "Whack that on your clit!"
I made Quim use the massager
Cos I knew it'd make her fanny feel tighter
It's times like this that I wish Geordie Steve would appear
In order to burn her pubes with his lighter
So yeah I fucked her then I came
On her arse and lower back
Quim the fat hoe from Facebook
Had at last got me in the sack
I'd spunked, I was done
No need to fuck her no more
I'd once again lowered myself
To fucking a big sweaty whore
I woke up the next morning
It had snowed loads over night
It was about 7.30 am
And had only just started to get light
But I wanted to fuck off
I'd had enough of this fat hoe
So I got dressed said goodbye
Then went out into the snow
I said "If you don't hear from me
It's because I got hyperthermia and died!"
"Well promise you'll come see me again soon"
"Yes of course I will Quim"
But you'll never guess what . . . . I lied!!

Magic Wand!

Behold the power of the magic wand
It's a vibrating sensual massager
It's the biggest most powerful one of its kind
Seriously you can't buy one any larger
Yes it's great for clits girls
Bitches they always cum when they use it
I slapped it on my bell end, it felt good
Now I often choose it
As an alternative to normal wanking
Yes the magic wand I have to thank
For allowing me to achieve the unthinkable
And have a lazy wank
No more frapping about frantically
Like I'm strangling a snake
I just stick the massager on to my nob
And within a few minutes it'll make
Me spunk like a fountain
All over my belly fur
I really recommend it
But now I'm not sure what I prefer
The lazy wank or the normal wank
Although this is not something over which I worry
Cos I guess it really all just depends
On whether or not I'm in a hurry!!

Mumpy Pumpy

Chris was all Mumped up
He was getting regular rumpy pumpy
He told me he was gonna save up
And get a joint mortgage with his bitch Mumpy
But that this was gonna take about six months
Hmm six more months of Mumps
With Chris acting Graham Norton gay
Every time he was with his creature from the flumps
"No I don't think I can deal with that
Sorry Chris you gotta move out quicker!!"
I mean I'd stopped smoking weed
And given up the liquor
Which rendered me defenceless
Against her judgemental Mumpy aura!
I didn't even like her in the same room as me
Yet strangely Chris seemed to adore her
So I weren't gonna fucking slag her off to him
But I really didn't want her in my yard
I had to be cruel to be kind
And with Mumpsface that weren't hard
I gave Chris two months to find a place
And I was really rather glad
When Chris told me him and his Mumpy hoe
Were gonna move in with her dad!!

Louie Spence

Going out with fat dull mump faces
Has massive consequences
And Chris was acting gayer
Than a bunch of Louie Spences!!

Shaven Hair

My hair was receding I couldn't save it
So at the end of January I chose to shave it
Did it look ok? I was in serious doubt
Cos it made my pointy ears stick out!!!

Are You Proud Of Me Martin

Here's a story from back in the day
From back in the Canterbury years
A story that explains the draw backs
Of mixing spirits, wines and beers!
I'd imagine it was a Thursday night
Cos on Thursday nights me and Martin would get passes
If we tried going out at the weekend
Jane and Barky would kick our arses
So let's just assume it was a Thursday
Cos weekends were mainly sherked
Martin had arranged a night out with his staff
He was manager of G.B.S. a shop where I once worked
I was now working in a different shop
But still popped in to see Martin on the regs
Sometimes I'd even help him tidy up
And hang clothes back up on their pegs
So all the staff at G.B.S. knew me
We were all quite familiar and good friends
Would this be just another night out in Canterbury?
"Tell me I want to know how this story ends"
Well you'll have to keep reading you impatient monkey
For now I'll keep you guessing
Anyway one of the people out that night was Lisa
A bird with whom I quite liked messing
She was a half oriental slitty eyed fuck
Oh and she had a brother called Paul
He was also half oriental
I didn't fancy him at all
So yeah we went out in Canterbury
Ended up in Churchill's a local Canterbury nightclub
It was 2 for 1 on drinks that night
And I'd already drunk loads in a pub
So 2 for 1 was asking for trouble
I was really knocking them back

I was getting more fucking shots in
Than that basketball player 'Shaq'
Obviously my recollection of what happened next
Is as you can hopefully appreciate quite blurred
The amount I'd drunk by this point
In the night was seriously absurd
We left Churchill's I know that much
And I don't think we'd gotten far
When Oriental Lisa's brother Oriental Paul
Pulled up in his brand new car
He'd only picked it up that day
It was a Golf G.T.I.
He said he'd give us a lift home
Can't remember why!
All I remember is sitting in the back
Making out with his sister Lisa
I couldn't string a sentence together
But I was sure I wanted a piece a
Her half oriental ying yang ass
So I began fingering her in the back
But then out of fucking no where
I spontaneously started to yack
All over Oriental Lisa
But more importantly all over Pauls new motor
He was fucking fuming mad
Unfortunately I didn't care one iota
Martin was apologising for me
I was a mess and Paul was very upset
Eventually Paul decided to find a garage
And hose down his interior with a water jet!
The next thing I remember
Is being in a 24 hour garage forecourt
Paul was spraying me with water
Pointing at sick saying "This mess is all your fault"
Then everyone went into the garage shop
I got out the car and found a bin
It seemed like a more suitable contraption
To go and be sick in

But somehow I pulled the bin over
And I was rolling around underneath it by pump three
When the others came out the garage shop
They gasped as I shouted "Martin are you proud of me?
I did this for you Martin!!"
I babbled as I tried to get to my feet
Martin was laughing his head off
Paul was still fucked off about his seat
He refused to let me get back in his car
His leather seats stank and they'd gone all waxy
Paul fucked off and left me there
Fortunately Martin had ordered us a taxi
I don't really remember the cab ride home
I think I got out and hurled into a hedge
"Are you proud of me Martin?" I asked again
"Yes mate of course I am that was the funniest thing
I've ever seen you're an absolute fucking ledge!!

Finishing Fifty Feels of Fuzz!

Quim was the final straw
Fucking birds like her was making me feel ill
It just made me regret wasting my energy
And using up a willy pill
No more plentyoffish.com
Not that that was my doing
I reckon that fat actress wheezy
The one who hated screwin
Had got the hump cos I'd mugged her off
When she really thought that she was great
Dumping posh actress hoes like mouldy bread
Is something posh actress hoes tend to hate
So yeah I reckon she reported me
To plenty of fish and got me barred
Like I gave a fuck I mean come on
Setting up a new account would not be hard
But I couldn't be arsed to do that
I had more important things to do
I had to finish Fifty Feels of Fuzz
My next book the Autorhymeography Part 2
Throughout January, February and most of March
All I did was write
Every spare minute of everyday
And every hour of every night
By mid-March it was written
Fifty Feels of Fuzz had been wrote
Now I had to find someone to type it up
Someone who needed to earn a swift pound note
I phoned a typist in Faversham
But she wanted a big fee
Plus she couldn't do it by my deadline
So she passed her friends number on to me
A woman by the name of Sue
I phoned this Sue and she was up for being my typist

Little did she know she'd be typing rhymes
About sluts, vagina's and my fist
I sent my pad of scribbled filth
To Sue along with a sum of cash
All that I had left to do
Was phone author house and tell them I'd had another bash
At writing and that by email
They'd soon be receiving my new manuscript
Titled 'Fifty Feels of Fuzz'
A book I told them that I hotly tipped
To win a fucking Booker prize
Cos it was that God damn fucking good
Just needed to get the publishing fee
Which I couldn't afford so I hoped my mother would
Let me pay a portion on her visa card
And help fund the rise of Pimpydee
She did bless her, love my mum
Plus I got a special deal, the next book I could publish free
Which is this book, the one you are reading now
This one in your hands
Confused? That's ok go ask someone
That fucking understands
What the difference is between self-publishing
And being published with an advance
Basically if you self-publish it costs you money
But it completely eliminates the chance
Of your book never being published
And I was never in this for the money
I just wanted to have my story out there
I wanted people to read about my life and find it funny
So yes in a way I suppose I cheated
My books got published that much is true
But that's because I paid to self-publish them
Which is something some people never knew
And Sue this lady I'd never met
Was who I paid to type book two
A different Sue typed my first book
Who in my last book I called Sucky Sue

And so it's kinda fucking funny
That this woman also had the name of Sue
That's Sucky Sue and now this lady
Who I'm calling Susan Number Two
Sue Two worked hard on Fifty Feels of Fuzz
But I kept finding errors and mistakes
Editing 300 plus pages of my rhyming filth
Well a lot of time that takes
But my Asperger's was off the chart
The need to complete fuzz was driving me insane
Felt like a million termites had climbed in to my head
And were all nibbling at my brain
I had to get the book out
I was close and I could feel it
Fifty Feels of Fuzz meant a lot to me
It was full of personal and real shit
Eventually I gave Sue Two the go ahead
To email the finished copy to Author House to print
And I emailed off to them my book cover
You should see it it is mint
It's me in my dogs head gimpmask
Encircled in a circular gold frame
On a black background with gold writing
Spelling out the title and my name
All my illustrations had been scanned and sent
Now all I had to do was chill out and wait
However Author House had big issues with my book
Causing a big delay to the expected release date
I had to change some company names
I couldn't use photos without getting consent
I couldn't have full frontal cartoon nudity
And all this red tape meant
Lots and lots of faffing about
And tweaking of my manuscript
By this point I was going nuts
Yes I think by now I'd flipped
Luckily it was around this time
That one of my employers B.F.K.

Asked if I'd be prepared to go and work in Brighton
If they found me a good hotel in which to stay
I was more than happy to oblige
I fancied an all-expenses paid break
Plus that sexy sloth Sid was staying in Brighton
Maybe of her complete advantage I could take
Sid? Sid the sloth she's in my last book
She's a sexy sloth for sure
But not a slut or an easy lay
She's a prick teasing kinda whore
However I really wanted to nob her
And still do oh so very much
I want to suffocate to death
With my face buried deep inside her crutch
So I was happy she was in Brighton
And gonna come out with me on the razzle
I didn't think I'd get to bang her
But maybe just maybe I could dazzle
Her with my awesome charisma
Maybe I could charm her into bed
Or maybe I could get her so pissed
She'd take me to the beach and give me head
Well you've got to be in it to win it
I'd got her out I had entered the lotto
I then proceeded to buy two bottles of wine
Gotta get this sloth hoe blotto
Me and Sid the sloth drank the wine
We then did lots of shots
Sid you fucking boss eyed sloth
For you I have the hots
We went to some random night club
But by now I was blind drunk
We kissed and canoodled
But I guess I'm not the kinda hunk
That Sid the sloth puts out for
Cos when we got back to my hotel
She said "I'm not staying Pimps!"
Which was probably just as well

Cos as soon as I got into my room
I started spinning out and feeling sick
I projectile vomited everywhere
So the fact is I doubt my dick
Would have been up to much
And all Sid would have been good for
Would've been to help me in the morning
Clean the pool of vomit off the floor
So yet again I didn't get to fuck Sid
Yet again her fanny proved elusive
But I will never give up one day I'll fuck Sid
I won't let this missed chance prove conclusive
One day Sid we're having sex
Maybe after you've shit out some kids you might cave in
Anyway fear not you Sloth
For you my heart I'll still be saving
One day we'll make sweet sweet love
It'll be like something outta romantic novel
Ha! Or if I win the Lotto jackpot
Then it'll be you phoning me to grovel
"Please Pimps I love you now you're rich
Now you have a mansion and a yacht!"
"Who is this?" "Sid the sloth!"
"Sid who? Sorry can't recall must have forgot!"
Yes Sid if I become a millionaire
Then your bum is in for a rocky ride
Payback for you rejecting my advances
All those times I tried
All those times I tried to woo you
To get you in the sack
For all those drinks I've brought you
Bitch I want my money back
Nah I don't! I like you
You can still be my slothy friend
But this aint it! It aint over Sid
Until my cocks balls deep in your rear end!
Ok where was I? Oh yes throwing up
In my hotel room in Brighton

I woke the next day ill surrounded by sick
Feeling glum but my mood was soon to lighten
For as I checked through my emails
I noticed one from my publisher Author House
It was the greatest it was fantastic
Like the start of Dangermouse
It was the news I had been waiting for
My book had gone to print and on its way
Was the 1st edition hard back copy
Finally all that hard work had come to pay
At last I could unleash the glorious front cover
On Facebook, have that mofos
Time to face some backlash
From worried ex's and a back catalogue of hoes
"What the fuck! You've done another book
What the fuck have you put about me?
You best not have used my actual name!
You know what I'll buy it just to see!"
Anyway that is how it happened
How I managed to do a second book
Fifty Feels of Fuzz
A lot of dedication it sure took
It's still available at Amazon and Waterstones
So if you don't own it buy it A.S.A.P.
I promise you will find it funny
Plus it'll mean more royalties for me!!

Blessed Are The Seahorses!

The front cover of Fifty Feels of Fuzz
To be honest looks satanic
Asperger Syndrome is a fucked up condition
It makes me go all manic
When I get a thought in my mind
I just can't let it go
I have to fucking do it
Or it'll do my nut in more than you could know!
After 'Fifty Feels of Fuzz' was published
And I had the first actual copy in my hand
One such thought popped into my head
These thoughts are sudden never planned
I thought 'hmm yes that front cover is dark and twisted
It looks good I really rate it'
But that's cos I have demonic tendencies
I'm sure if I was a Christian I would hate it!
Yeah if I was a God fearing church goer
I'd have definitely tried to ban 'Fifty Shades of Grey'
'Fifty Feels of Fuzz' looks twice as wrong
If I were a Christian I'd want it banned straight away
Light bulb! I had a plan I'd become a Christian
Start a fellowship, call them the church of pink and pastel blue
Get some t shirts printed with that written on the front
Then what my Christian fellowship could do
Is start a ban this book campaign
I'd get leaflets made then start protesting my own book
Ten thousand leaflets I had printed up
And they were designed to make people want to look
At what the fuck they'd just been handed
'Ban this book' then under that an image of my front cover
Holy Mary mother of Christ
"What in God's name is this my Christian brother?"
'Do not buy this book' it reads
'It is trying to corrupt innocent young people

Don't fall for it, don't follow the trend
Don't be one of the sheeple
This book is full of vulgarity
And contains perverse sexual acts
It's being used as a tool to brain wash you
You need to know the facts
This book should not be purchased
It should be banned with immediate affect'
"Blessed are the seahorses" that was my slogan
And it was pretty easy to perfect
Say it with me 'In God we trust
Blessed are the seahorses praise the Lord amen
Thou shalt not take the name of the Lord thy God in vain"
That's commandment number 3 out of the 10
My marketing campaign sure was blasphemous
But holy fuck it would be funny
So I had the leaflets and t shirts made
Which cost a fair amount of money
Now my idea had become reality
But was I risking Gods mighty wrath
I'd already broken two commandments this would be one more
Which equals three if you do the math
So I looked up to heaven for some guidance
And spoke to God in the hope that he would hear
"Is it ok to pretend to be a Christian to promote my book?"
"Cool by me!" God responded "In fact it's an excellent idea!"

Ban the Book!

So with the all clear from the Lord Almighty
I put on a t shirt and went out in town to flyer
"I'm trying to ban this vile book" I said to the public
But these days I'm not much of a liar
I couldn't keep a straight face
When people quizzed me about my faith
So rather than have to lie to them
What I did instead to be safe
Was just hand them a leaflet
Then walk off saying "Blessed is the seahorse"
Did I feel a bit shady doing that?
Damn right I did of course
Atheism is one thing
But pretending to be a Christian is naughty is it not?
"Hey God I'm still promoting Christianity
Don't send me to hell it looks too hot
I was handing my leaflets out—in Canterbury
One of the holiest cities on the map
If the Arch Bishop of Canterbury had seen me
I'd have been in a ton of crap . . . .
Fortunately he didn't!
I gave out leaflets all day long
Remember God told me that it was a good idea
Although there's a chance I got that wrong
Perhaps it wasn't God after all
But my schizophrenia talking to me
When you're a paranoid schizophrenic
Sometimes the voices in your head aren't who they claim to be
Well anyway someone told me to do it
And it was too late now to care what God might think
I was handing out leaflets with a 'Christian' t shirt on
Which by the way was pastel fucking pink!!

We the pink and pastel blue christian fellowship association
would like you to help us

BAN THIS BOOK

On the 7th of june 2013 a book called 'FIFTY FEELS OF FUZZ' went on general
sale across the UK... This book is readily available from stockists such as
Amazon.com, Waterstones.co.uk, WH Smiths.co.uk, Authorhouse.com... ect... This
book just like 'FIFTY SHADES OF GREY' is nothing but a satanic attempt to
corrupt the minds of young impressionable females and a covert operation by the
shadowey elites to decensorsize the general populas to extreme acts of sexual
vulgarity! Do not be a sheep. Do not buy this book... Infact help us 'The pink and
pastel blue christian fellowship' to get it pulled from the shelves... Write to your MP
or join us on facebook at 'pinkandpastelblue chritianfellowshipassociation'...
blessed are the seahorses :) xxxxxxxxxx

Leaflets

I had to get those leaflets out
So dressed in my Christian t shirt
I spent the next few weeks
Placing them in takeaways and tattoo parlours
Pubs, clubs, hairdressers,
Tanning salons and boutiques!!

Tree

You stand so tall and proud
Your leaves are big and green
You are by far and away
The most impressive tree I've ever seen!

What the Tree

Why halfway through this book of filth
Is there a random poem about a tree
Because my friend you need to understand
That I'm the unpredictable Pimpydee!!

Surprise Cock Faces!

We had arranged it months in advance
Ben would fly over from Sweden
And be Steve and Lesley's surprise engagement gift
And all I was now needin
Was a great big cardboard box
To stash Ben in on the day
Which I got from a local shop
Just around the way
On the evening of the big engagement dinner
Me and Martin met up with Ben
Stashed him in the giant box
Tied it with a bow and ribbon and then
We left it outside the restaurant
Where everyone was already seated
Me and Martin went in, said "Hi" to Steve and Les
Actually every one of their guests we greeted
Then we informed Steve and Lesley
That someone had left a big present outside by the door
Quite a few people went out to take a look
Shame it wasn't more
Cos what happened next was epic
It was almost too fucking spectacular to believe
As Lesley went to open the gift
After being instructed to by Steve
The box fucking exploded
And out leapt a Benjamin Beal
"Surprise cock faces!" shouted Ben as he got out
"I'm here for your engagement meal!"

Ben In A Box

Lesley began undoing the ribbon
She was about to get a big surprise
"Kaboom!!" A Ben in a box
No wonder she had tears in her eyes!!

A.F.

Ben my friend we go way back
Remember when we'd get Kev to attack
Anyone we wanted him to
Animal Foundation Crew!!

Ben

Hey Ben do you remember this
21 nights on the piss
Sleeping in Ramsgate outside that 2nd hand furniture store
Cos we'd got so pissed we couldn't walk no more
Under upturned settees we created beds
Crazy drunken sleepy heads
A woman woke us early morn
We stank of booze and looked forlorn
Then back to my house we staggered
We walked in still pissed, looking haggard
Which was when my dad gave us a stern talking to
"You boys drink far too much it's not good for you!"
Then he made some daft comment
About your parent's divorce which sent
You into an angry rage
My dad hadn't stopped to consider your age
We were still only about eighteen
He realised he'd been far too mean
So he went outside with you to apologise
Well done pops that was wise
Then after all that kafuffle
After your feathers he'd managed to ruffle
He said "I expect you boys could do with a drink
Here's two cold beers!" then with a cheeky wink
Said "Seriously you boys are drinking far too much
I'll let you off this time you've had a touch!"
I gotta say the whole thing turned out better
Then I'd been hoping
"Hey Ben lets go into town and wait for the pubs to open!"

Sometimes When I Open My Mouth Shit Comes Out!

In 5th Avenue a nightclub long since gone
I did something only heard of in mythology
It's pretty gross so I'm gonna say sorry now
Call it an upfront heartfelt apology
See me and Ben had drunk a lot of vodka
To be precise vodka, ice and coke
(Remember what I'm about to tell you
Is Gospel truth and not a joke)
Anyway after drinking eight or nine vodka cokes
I suddenly felt sick
I ran into the nightclub toilets
And I don't know why I chose to pick
A sink to throw up into but I did
Then something really vile ensued
Instead of throwing up vomit I threw up shit
It was like I'd orally poo poo'ed
A big log of dark brown substance
Came up and out my throat like a big turd
I was taking a dump out of my mouth
How fucked up and absurd
Having forced this mouth turd out
I looked at it in the sink
The big log of dark brown crap
Had now began to stink
I washed my mouth out with lots of water
This experience really fucking spun me out
I bet you didn't think shitting out your mouth was possible
Well I can assure you it is without a doubt!!

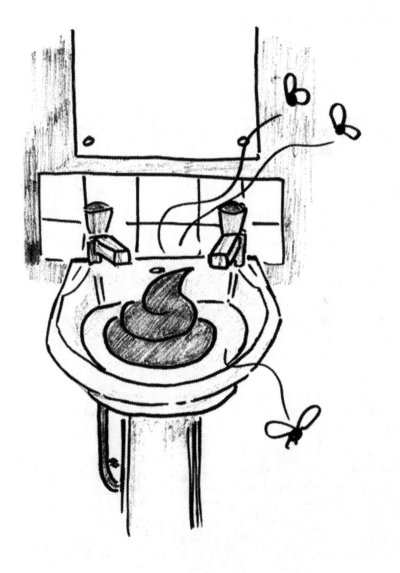

Bad Grandad!

My granddad on my father's side
I never met cos he died
Way before I came along
To him I dedicate this song
Grandad Grandad
My Dad said you were a git
I've seen a photo of you
I've studied it
You look like a dodgy man
I'd have to say
Grandad Grandad
You live on in my D.N.A.
Genetics mean you are a part of me
And now I understand
Why I am the way I am
It's cos of the dodgy granddad strand
Of D.N.A. and it's possible
That you are one of the voices in my head
The one that tells me to do bad things
I'm blaming you for this life I've led
Grandad Grandad
I reckon you were probably a right sod
I expect you ruled the roost
With an iron rod
You drank and smoked and gambled
You were a right old Jack the lad
But without you there'd be no me
Cos you helped create my Dad!!!

Busy Grandma

I don't know much about Dads mum
My Dad never mentioned her in his tales
All I know is she shat out a lot of kids
And lived somewhere in Wales!!

Uncle Kenny

I've got a load of uncles on my Dad's side
I don't even know how many
The only one I've ever met
Is my long lost Uncle Kenny!

No Show Bros!

I've got two half-brothers in theory
Although I've not seen or heard from them
Since I was small
They've made no attempt to contact me
And I've made no attempt at all
To contact them, fuck um
Their loss! It sure don't bother me
They're just two half-brothers I don't know
Where as I am Fuzzman A.K.A. The Mighty Pimpy Dee!

They Rape Seahorses

It was the last night of Folk Week
It had been a week of total fun
But I hadn't handed any leaflets out
Now some work had to be done
So I asked Matt if he would help me
He was up for spreading the message of my fellowship
I had shit loads of leaflets in my bag
And I was ready to let rip
We had a few beers outside the pub
Whilst handing out leaflets to passers by
"You're trying to ban Fifty Feels of Fuzz?"
"Yes" I'd say, then they'd ask me why
"Cos I'm a massive Christian believer
And the content in that book is so blasphemous!"
Which is the point when they would 'tease me'
I felt like Pliers and Chakademus!!
I'd be like "Really we are born again
And to us Christianity really means a lot
This book uses the Lord our Gods name in vain
Therefor condone it we do not!
It uses over two thousand expletives
And it encourages unnatural sexual experimentation damn it
This is the devils work and just like Fifty Shades of Grey
Down people's throats they try to ram it
So we the Pink and Pastel Blue Christians
Are trying to stop it from being sold
Especially to young impressionable females
Who are under eighteen years old!!"
Matt and I handed lots of leaflets out
But we were also getting drunk
By about 10.30 pm at night
At least six pints we'd sunk
And by 11 pm the Christian act
Was starting to wear thin

We had a lot of fun with it
Ridding slutty hoes of all their sin
By using the same trick the Jesus Army
Used on me and Ben all those years ago
I'd put my hand on a girls shoulder
Look up to God and start to pray for the dirty hoe
"Hear me Lord this is Chardonnay
Forgive her for her sins for she is sorry
She didn't mean to suck that geezer off
In the back of his fucking lorry
Show her the way, please guide her
The world is full of wolves she's just a lamb!"
The girls were feeling genuine guilt ha ha
They didn't know the whole thing was a sham
Remarkable when you consider that "Do you love seahorses?"
Was what Matt had now figured he should ask
"Yes I love seahorses why is that?"
"Well see that dude on the leaflet in the mask?"
"Yeah" "Well he fucking rapes seahorses
And this book tells people how to rape them too
And we have every reason to think everything in this book
Is all 100% fucking true
So we are saying don't buy this book
If you love seahorses you'll take a leaflet and pass it on
Otherwise there's a chance that by twenty fifteen
All the seahorses will be gone
People were not convinced we were Christians now
And some people didn't like what we were doing
"Fucking book dogs head seahorse porn
Seahorse rapes and screwin!"
Yes my religious preaching wasn't working
And I was proper drunk and laggin
Staggering around Broadstairs spillin my pint
With half an unlit fag in
Was not a good advertisement
For the church of Pink and Pastel Blue
So I walked back to my mums house to go to bed
As it was the smartest thing that I could do

But just as I got to my mums
My phone started to ring
It was Dappy "Where are you?" he asked
"Cos I wanna do that Christian thing!"
I'd told Daps that I wanted him to help
But it was only now that he'd made contact
"I've got my pink God t shirt on" he said
Apparently it was just leaflets that he lacked
"Come and meet me at Thanet College
I'm picking up some tasty Mandy!"
"Fuck it ok then but I'll need some too!"
Thinking a dab of M.D.M.A. right now would sure be handy
I met up with Daps and his crew
Dangerous Dave and his brother Kenny
"Have you got lots of leaflets left?"
"I've got some but I'm fucked if I know how many!"
They were on it straight away
Giving out leaflets here and there
Dangerous Dave by coincidence handed one
To my daughter Moofy Bear
So she came and found me
Said "Hi Dad" and gave it back
These things can happen when ya kids in their mid-teens
Luckily enough I weren't on crack
My daughter was on her way home with her friend
And I was off to get drugs with Dappy
I was really drunk and tired
I needed that dabby dabby dabby
Did half a gram of Mandy
Then went to the beach
Me and Daps were fucking spanked in no time
Cos we'd done half a ticket each
There were loads of youngsters on Viking Bay
All drinking and getting leen
But you know what the last thing they expected was?
The one thing I guarantee they'd never seen
Was two guys in Christian fellowship t shirts
Drinking, smoking weed and doing spasticated gurns

Accompanied by Dangerous Dave and his brother
Kenny who looks like Mr Burns
The Mandy was kicking my arse
I couldn't help it I had to hurl
Which is when I felt a comforting arm around me
It belonged to a young girl
She was about 18 or 19
She was like "Are you ok?
You're a bloody Bible basher
How did you end up in this bad way?"
"I think one of my congregation
Spiked my lemonade Panda Pop with drugs!"
The nice girl felt well bad for me
And insisted on giving me lots of hugs
Normally I would have tried to pull her
But I was far too cunted to speak
There I was in a God t shirt off my nut being sick
On the last night of Folk Week!
I stayed down the beach til sunrise
I was sat by a bonfire playing a harmonica I'd acquired
A fat bird sat across from me, I could see her cunt
But the drugs had worn off now and I was tired
So I stopped playing the harmonica
(The harmonica makes such an awesome sound)
The leaflets had all been handed out
 But from the look of Broadstairs most had been chucked upon the
  ground
Never mind! It was home time for this Christian
I needed my bed and lots of rest
I'd prayed for several drunken sluts
And lots of seahorses had been blessed!!!

Sheen

Charlie Sheen legend
But imagine if
Someone turned him into powder
And sold it for you to sniff!

Sniffing Sheen

Best legal high I've ever seen
£10 for a sachet of Charlie Sheen
So Matt and I bought a bag to share
Sniff Charlie Sheen if you dare!!

Notting Hill

Come with me if you will
To a carnival at Notting Hill
Cha cha cha chee chee chee
Pollen, Sid, Matt and me!
Curried goat rice and pea
Jerk chicken, fruit punch for free
Good times bus, Norman Jay
Noz balloons, sunny day
Crazy dreads off their heads
Feeding us neat rum
Good fun we had, aint you glad
I persuaded you all to come!!

Check Ya Shelf Before Ya Wreck Ya Shelf!

Poor old Matt, got some flack
For making Sid get on her hands and knees
But he only did that
So he could use her back
To skin up on! "Yo geez!!"
Said a home boy walking by
To his pal "Check that guy
He's got that hoe proper in enslavement
Man's doing well for himself
He's turned that hoe into a skinning up shelf
Look she's on all fours on the dirty pavement!!

The Chinese Whore and the Butt Plug!

I'd been drinking beer and smoking weed
And I had the fucking horn
And I had a spare £60 quid
So rather than wank to porn
I booked myself a Chinese hoe
'Why the fuck not' I said to myself
They should prescribe Chinese whores
For free on the National Health
So you feel stressed out and up tight
Here take one hooker every other day
But I didn't have a prescription
£60 quid I'd have to pay
So I thought I'd really go for it
And take the electro stim butt plug
Some guys probably pay Chinese hookers
Just to talk to them and hug
But I'm not one of those guys
I'm a little more perverse
The vibrating massager was kind of acceptable
But this gadget was clearly much worse
And this particular Chinese hooker
Was not impressed by my device
She didn't embrace the idea of using it
Like she embraced the idea of egg fried rice
As soon as she saw it she made it clear
That she wasn't gonna let me stick it in her
"That's ok you can stick it up my arse then
Your loss now I'm the winner!!"
So I made her stick it in my rectum
And turn the power up from green to red
"This feels great!!" I told her
"I'm happy it's in my bum instead!!"
For the record it actually does feel pretty good
You wouldn't think 500 volts

Inside your anus would feel so pleasurable
But its pulsations and its jolts
Make your arsehole feel fucking funky
Your dick will get harder than ever before
Which is why it was at this point
I stuck my cock into the Chinese whore
I began to fuck her doggy style
Fuck China don't join um fucking beat um
I was batting for team dog
Cos in China people eat um!
I was enjoying this experience
Fucking with the butt plug up my butt
The voltage kicking out from that thing
Could probably trigger a power cut!
Anyway I was getting right into it
And I was just about to cum
When the fucking thing started slipping
Then popped right out of my bum
It landed on the back of the hookers leg
Causing her to jump out of her yellow skin
I went to pick the butt plug up
I was gonna pop it right back in
But I forgot how lethal it is to touch
It's literally fucking shocking
Which is why when I went to pick it up
Whilst attempting to re-stick my cock in
I panicked and threw it up in the air
It had zapped me fucking bad
But when it fell it landed on the hookers foot
Which made the hooker mad
"Oowww!! That fucking thing turn it off!!"
The Chinese hooker yelped
Which I did, then put it away
And said "Sorry couldn't be helped!
It's very very powerful but I promise you
It feels great once it's fucking in!"
The Chinese whore did not believe me though
She wanted me to throw it in the bin

Obviously I didn't fucking do that
I put it safely into my jacket pocket
"You're not right in the head!" said the hooker
"Well until you try it you can't knock it!!"
Anyway I carried on fucking the Chinese hoe
All be it without any electrodes zappin my ring
Maybe in hind sight it wasn't
The most appropriate device to bring
But if you don't ask you don't get
I didn't get but at least I asked
This Chinese hooker was either lazy or a prude
In that she just couldn't be arsed
Or wouldn't be arsed with a butt plug
Or for that matter arsed by my cock
If I'd been a nasty cunt
I'd have beat her with a wok
But I'm not nasty I'm a lovely guy
So I made sweet love to her all gentle
Five minutes earlier when I zapped her foot
She'd been going ape shit mental
But now she'd calmed down thankfully
And she made sure I got my happy ending
She said she hated the butt plug though
So to her I guess it I won't be lending!
"Goodbye darling" I said as I left
"Goodbye thank you darling" she replied
Her arse hole could have been like her foot
And her egg rice i.e. fucking fried
But instead I took one for the team
And it felt much better than you'd think
So yeah 10 points for team dog
And no points what so ever for team chink
Anyway don't let it be said
That I can dish it out but I can't take it
Not trying out my own expensive sex toys
Would be more stupid than girls that feel the need to fake it
Right ok I think that's all
Another Chinese whore story bites the dust

I wonder if I clean that butt plug with soap and water
But don't bother to dry it will it rust?
I dunno! Best I don't take the risk
I'm gonna go now n fucking dry it
Then put it on fucking ebay
£80 if you'd like to buy it!
Who am I kidding I can't sell it
It's got sentimental meaning
Oh what stories that thing could tell
In fact I think it needs an extra cleaning
So I'm gonna go and clean it
To it I shall attend
This is it the story's finished
Seriously, the end!!!

Oxhoe Cubes!

I knew one of your sisters
Was dumb but fucking fit
I picked the other sister
Ugly and dumb as fucking shit
She had a slim physique
And her hair was long
But everything else about her
Was seriously wrong
Stupidly I booked me and her a table
At my favourite eating place
Good restaurant for impressing fit birds
Wasted on this fucking council face!!

Mmmm Bisthoe!!!

Dumbest cunt I've ever met
However the expensive fucking meal she et
So I dragged her stupid arse to mine
Then downed a bottle of Rose wine
I was gonna fuck this circus freak
She had psoriasis on each bum cheek
Not the most attractive rear
She asked if I could get her some gear
I said "No" then it came to me
Chris had stashed some shit Mandy
In a wooden box on my kitchen shelf
So I figured I would help myself
I mean it had been there for ever
To take it now would not be clever
So I gave it to this crusty slut
This fucked up hoe with the scabby butt
She woofed it down the whole g
Didn't even give none to me
Not that I wanted any
I just wanted to bum this Benny
I stuck my cock in her dopey gob
Shut up you mong and suck my nob
Yes just cos this div had no class
Didn't mean I weren't gonna fuck her arse
But first cos I'm quite polite
I fucked her cunt, cunt weren't tight
So I got out the electrostim butt plug
And shoved it in this hood rat mug
Turned it up to full zap
Well done slut clap clap clap
Fucked her in the cunt some more
Then figured I should bum the whore
I fucked her arse of course I did
But then the dozy flid

Let her bowels release some dung
Her shit slipped out like words off my tongue
Nasty bum gravy nobody likes that
Bum gravy puddles that bitch shat
I said "Well that weren't wise
You sort it out I'm going beddy bies!"
Then I rolled over and held my nose
I fucking hate bum gravy hoes!!

Conspiracies

Right! After my outburst in my last book
I feel I should update you
If you think I'm a fucking loon
Don't worry I don't hate you
But I want to take this opportunity
To tell you where I stand
I'm gonna say stuff so near the mark
It'll get this third book banned!
Ok let's start at the beginning
Back when I was five
And having proper realistic dreams
In which it appeared I'd be alive
To witness Armageddon
My dreams would depict an apocalyptic scenario
"Perhaps you were playing too much space invaders
On your fucking Atari 2600 bro!"
Nope it weren't cos of that! This was cryptic
It's something in me I've always known
And as the years have passed
The fucking feelings grown!
Ok moving on to Terry Wogan
The infamous Wogan Show
When David Icke first mentioned reptilians
Twenty three years ago
Now that sure got me thinking
Thinking even more
I sure as hell didn't believe the reasons we were given
For the first fucking Iraq war
Didn't believe Diana's death was an accident
Didn't believe 9/11 was Osama
Didn't trust Bush or Tony Blair
Didn't fall for all the hype about Obama
Watched loads of conspiracy documentaries
About U.F.O's and the N.W.O.

The moon landing, aliens
And all of this made my paranoia grow
But in between all of this
I was fucking living my life
I was dealing with all sorts of stuff
Work and marriage strife
I didn't have the time nor the desire
To research conspiracies I had other stuff to do
However my intrigue didn't disappear
I still questioned what was and wasn't true
Like why did 'they' kill J.F.K.?
Was Michael Jackson actually killed?
'They' don't really care about us! Who's they?
Hmm well I bet that 'they' were thrilled
When MJ (he sang Thriller) snuffed it
He knew too much just like Diana
Both of them got taken out
In a dodgy fucking manner!
Then came the whole Splodgey thing
That fiasco with the fake baby
Which was when I developed actual sixth sense
"Were you telepathic?" "Dunno for certain, maybe!"
Then I discovered the Icke iphone app
That app seemed to fit all the conspiracies together
And that's when I got sucked right in
And went fucking hell for leather
Watching every single conspiracy video
Through hundreds I sat and sifted
I re watched that Wogan Icke interview
And noticed a studio audience member shape shifted
That Wogan interview subsequently disappeared
Leaving me fucking spun
Which is the moment yes that was the moment
When my reptilian man hunt first begun
I watched loads about reptoids
Ickes stuff was the best
Then came Rik clay and the Olympics
"Seriously Fuzz give it a rest!"

Yep lots of people were sick of me
Preaching all the fucking time
Well guess what I'm back on it
That's why I've done this rhyme!
See the Olympics were satanic
Clearly obvious when your minds awakened
When all your indoctrination
You've shrugged off and forsaken!
I watched Jessie Venturer on Conspiracy Theories!
I watched Alex Jones on Info Wars
I watched documentary after documentary
Instead of all ya T.O.W.I.E.'s and Geordie Shores
I snared Gareth Icke as a Facebook friend
On a quest to find my missing studio lizard
The fact that that Wogan Show vanished off the web
Was even weirder than Eddie Izzard!!
Still no sign of that interview
That mystery continues to this day
And the Ickes lack of willingness to acknowledge it
Is one of the main reasons I would say
That my Icke trust dropped down a bit
Cos I just couldn't work it out
Surely if no one believed your lizard theory
And you had a way to prove it beyond all doubt
You'd want to do so wouldn't you?
Never mind! That didn't change the fact
That I was certain reptilian shape shifters existed
It was just solid evidence that I lacked
So where do I stand on all this now?
Well Ickes predictions continue to unfold
WW3 is imminent, the world's economy is doomed
And from what we're being told
It would appear the George Orwell classic
'1984' really was prophetic
Microchippin, surveillance, free speech gone
Let's face it western civilisation is on the whole pathetic
Too dumbed down to rebel too mind manipulated
Too encased in their own prism

To notice as they acquiesce
And help build the walls to their own prison
See when something is so in your face
It's called hidden in plain sight
Unfortunately I only see ahead
Humanities continued dismal plight
Then one day a guy called Donald Marshall
Popped up on a David Icke message board
Saying that Dave weren't telling the full story
And that he was a sell-out fraud
So I checked out this Donald Marshall dude
He claims the reptoids are called Vrill
How deep underground military bases or D.U.M.B.'s
Have cloning centres where he has to spend time against his will
Apparently the lizard people aint shape shifters
They are an ancient prehistoric race
Dinosaur in origin, not that bright
Smelly, with a nasty lizardy face
Only the upper echelons of high society
Are allowed to know that they exist
There's a secret few that interact with them
But they're on one fucking exclusive list
See the Vrill produce a parasite
Which fires out of their head into a human's eye
The human then becomes a host to the Vrill parasite
And this apparent true explanations why
The Ickes didn't want to investigate my lizard man
Because he was more than likely a Vrill host
And the Ickes can't mention them cos that's the rules
So who do I believe the most?
David Icke the truth granddaddy?
Who talks of interdimensional archons but wont
Talk about human cloning centres or clones
And I can tell you David definitely don't
Ever mention Hitler's interest in the Vrill
Or this other possible reason why
Just about every music artist to make it big
Poses for photos covering one eye

Ga Ga, Jay Z, Beyonce, Shady, go check it out
And you'll see that I'm not mental
It gets to the point where it's so ridiculous
It simply can't just be coincidental
They must do it for a reason
And Don's parasite in the eye reason seems legit
Why do they all cover one eye?
It's some proper fucked up shit
Now admittedly this Donald dude could be a wacko
I mean his story is almost silly
Look him up check out his website
But don't go dismissing what he says willy nilly
Because as time goes by more and more evidence
Appears to back up his claims
Fuck I'd love to know the actual truth
Before this world goes up in flames!
So where am I in all of this?
I'll tell you where I'm at
YouTube or Google human cloning and Mkultra mind control
And see what you make of that
Then search for rappers and the Illuminati
Or Illuminati sacrifices and dead musicians
Look at Illuminati and Hollywood symbolism
Then search 'Freemasons in powerful positions'
Listen to Rosanne Barr talking about mind control
Or Charlie Sheens views on 9/11
Watch any one of a number of documentaries
About the hidden facts surrounding London 7/7
Listen to President Kennedy's anti Illuminati speech
And what M.J. said about 'they' destroying our planet
Watch the interviews after his murder
The interviews with his sisters Latoya and Janet
'They' killed him 'they' did it
But Janet and Latoya refuse to say
Who exactly 'they' actually is
Paris Jackson his daughter also speaks of 'they'
The Bilderberg Group, Bohemian Grove
Skull and Bones, Freemasonic rule

Watch all the stuff about ancient civilisations
The Anunnaki, man you'd have to be a fool
Not to believe something's amiss
What is the top secret stuff filed under classified?
Why is it all the famous people that spoke out
Against this shit subsequently died?
Lennon, Hendrix, Bob Marley, 2 Pac, M.J.
J.F.K., Malcolm X to name but a few
Go ahead look up what they said about the illuminati
Everything they said is true
So to clarify where I stand is this
I believe some force is pushing a dark agenda
Someone or something is really doing all it can
To try and put an end ta
This planets natural eco system
And the human race as it once was
And I think, in fact I'm almost convinced
That they are doing this because
They want the earth's environment
To be like them smelly, ugly and grey
Then perhaps when the atmosphere is devoid of oxygen
The reptoid creatures can come out their holes to play
Maybe they've been planning this for hundreds of years
Fact is I'm probably never really gonna know
I'm not a top ranking Freemason or a Royal
Or a billionaire banker so
I'm gonna have to wait for shit to reach the point
When it's all revealed that's when folks will want advice
Cos they're being forced to microchip their babies
And are finally realising they're paying the price
For not believing any of this was happening
And now have no choice but to obey
"I told you so, I told you so!"
Is what you'll hear me say!
So yes this is where I stand right now
I think there's most likely something lizardy at work
Not knowing for fucking certain though
Is driving me berserk

And what winds me up, what grinds my gears
Is that a select elite group do fucking know
It's like when someone says "I know something
It's really bad but I can't tell you though!"
Frustrating isn't it
Well all this conspiracy stuff frustrates me
That's why I'm moaning
But mark my words one thing that will be exposed
Is clone centres and human cloning
Fuck it I could rhyme about this
Forever and a day
So I'll stop here cos I've said
Basically everything I think I want to say
Go investigate this stuff yourselves
Take the time to research it then decide!
I can't make you believe in lizard people
But I sure have fucking tried!!

The Treasure Cunters

Never judge a book by its cover
Never judge a bird's cunt by her body
Sometimes birds with a lovely frame
Have a cunt that's rather shoddy
And sometimes birds with shocking frames
Are hiding pussies of real high calibre
Just cos a birds got saggy tits and has two kids
Don't mean you shouldn't pull out your pork sword like Excalibur
You never know what pussy a bitch has got
Until you get to meet it
This one fat saggy hoe had a pussy so fucking nice
Very few other pussies I've met beat it!
Sure this girl weren't a size 8
Sure her tits had gone all droopy
She weren't a small yellow bird like Woodstock
She was more of a big white dog like Snoopy
But she'd made the effort to come to Whitstable
She'd even paid for the cab
No matter what cunt she had in her pants
I was going in like Andy Mcnab!
I mean I wasn't very optimistic
She was the mother of two young nippers
She had saggy tits and bingo wings
And her breath smelt of chicken dippers
So you can imagine my excitement
When I pulled her cacks off to find
A nice neat tucked in pussy
"Nice pussy" "Why thank you you're so kind!"
"No really love I'm in actual shock
Your pussy it's actually fucking amazing!"
For about ten minutes I was transfixed
At it I just couldn't stop a'gazin!
It was a struggle to get two fingers in
It was practically unused

Darnel sanchez

"But you've had two children recently" I said
"Your pussy's unscathed and I'm confused!"
"Too posh to push, I had two caesareans!"
Just got a tummy scar that's all!"
"Even so your pussy is so tight inside!"
"That's cos my ex's penis was real small!"
Well there you go you never know
Always expect the unexpected that's what I've learned
You can be pleasantly surprised if you expect the worst
Especially where fannies are concerned
Just cos a birds a fatty or has kids
In those knickers you should still hunt
Trust me this plump saggy titted single mum
Was worth her weight in cunt!
I really enjoyed fucking that pussy
I think I cum about four times
Which is at least double the amount I usually spunk
In most of my other sex story rhymes
So to you the girl in question
Give your fanny a round of applause for it gave me pleasure
And to all you guys that like a nice cunt to fuck
Remember only those of you that search everywhere
Will find that secret pussy treasure!!!

Tax-E Driver!

I figured I'd go see Pave and Dap
N give um a book each, aint I kind
I went to their flat at 3 pm on a Saturday
Not quite sure what messiness I would find!
Well Daps was out but Pave was in
He'd been up all night and was still bang on it
There was some big ol' taxi driver there too
Saying "I got a ticket left do you want it?"
Hmm well there were two hot girls there too
And some other funny geezer
He kept saying "E's are really good!"
"Yeah I fucking know that Ebenezer!"
This was a lot of messiness
For 3 o'clock in the afternoon
So I bought the ticket (wrap of coke)
Off of the massive taxi driver loon
Sniffed that, then Dap turned up
The hoes left and we sniffed more gear
The big taxi driver and his pal
Wanted us to all go out in Pramsgate for a beer
But first he thought it would be a good idea
To call someone and get some E's
They arrived he munched two so did his mate
I had half of one as I planned on getting some z's
As I had Marie the next morning
So I had that half and that was it
Glad I did cos within 20 minutes
The taxi drivers mates night began to go shit
He threw up then passed out on the floor
To be fair he looked dead
The big taxi dude had no sympathy
And kept smacking him in the head
Then he started being sick too
Pave got him a bucket

Daps was proper worried now
"I'm gonna ring an ambulance fuck it!"
"Don't do that just yet Daps
Let's see if he comes around!"
Admittedly at this point he was choking on his own tongue
Lying flat out on the ground
And that was the moment I decided
To give Pave and Daps their books "Here take these"
I signed them and wrote 'When I signed this book
I was surrounded by people dying from dodgy E's!'
(Fitting really what with my books content!)
Then I went downstairs and went to sleep
The taxi driver dude was still throwing up
His mate was still a motionless unconscious heap!
Best way to deal with that kinda carnage
Is to run away and hide
Pave and Daps had signed copies of my book
And as of yet no one had died!
So it was time for Fuzzy to disappear
Whilst the going was good
I'd survived another night in Pramsgate
At Daps and Paves deep in the fucking hood!!!

The Lumpy Ball Blues!

A few days after the night at Folk Week
After the M.D.M.A. ban the book Christian fellowship campaign
I noticed a swelling to my left testicle
My stupid nuts had gone kaput again
I figured it must be that pesky hematoma
It must have moved into someplace new
I presumed the swelling would go down
But for now there weren't much I could do
As the weeks passed my ball felt more lumpy
Maybe this was nothing to do with my hematoma moving about
It wasn't a fucking S.T.D. I'd not had sex in ages
I couldn't work it out
Please God don't let it be ball cancer
I really didn't need this drama
But the more I thought about it the worse it seemed
Bloody hell I think this could be karma
It's karma for my dig at Mr Gnome
Splodge's step dad from my last book
He had had cancer of the testicle
I knew it would come back on me cos I took
The piss out of his misfortune
When I said he couldn't be a dad
Cos he'd had one of his bollocks off
That he'd only got one nad
And now this was my comeuppance
Karma you're so so cruel
The lump was fucking uncomfortable
And if I didn't get it checked by a G.P. I'd be a fool
So I phoned up the doctors surgery

Darnel sanchez

But they couldn't see me that day too busy
I was convinced that I had cancer
I'd gotten myself into a right old tizzy
But I couldn't make an appointment the next day
Didn't matter how anxious I was feeling
For I was off to London the next morning
For a few days to work in Ealing!!

What The Fuck Is Hematoma?

Ok back in my first book
You can read about my nasty mishap
But don't you dare laugh at my misfortune
Or I'll give you a fucking bitch slap
See as I was climbing through a window
I slipped and fell and smashed my nuts
Right onto the base of the window frame
You know the bit onto which the window shuts
This caused my nut sack to swell up really bad
Into a big purple cannon ball
And when the swelling went down weeks later
I began to see the true extent of the damage from my fall
For where I once had had two testicles
I now seemed to have three
Each one was the same size and shape
But how in God's name could that be?
Martin took me to the hospital
To see a ball specialist whose job it was to look
At my ball bag but he was confused
His head he scratched and shook
"I'm sending you for an ultrasound scan"
I had to go see a nurse
Who smeared cold goop on my scrotum
Could things get any worse?
Up on to the screen appeared my three balls
Two white and one jet black
The two white ones were my testicles
The other was where blood had formed a sack
"That's called a hematoma
It will decrease in size eventually!" she said
And it did but it took years and years
Which brings us up to the last poem you just read
See this hematoma was now much much smaller
The size of a very small frozen pea

Darnel sanchez

Sometimes I could feel it inside with my balls
But sometimes I had no idea where it could be
Which is why I thought it was possible
That it had lodged itself somewhere dumb
Where it could cause some kind of irritation
Maybe it was causing inflammation each time I cum
Could it be doing something really bad?
I had no way of telling
All I knew was I was starting to worry
About the fucking lump and swelling!!

St James Park Life!

The last time I'd stayed in Ealing
I'd fucked Troll Face and lost a grand
So I wondered what would happen this time
I wondered what fate had planned
What fate had in store was just absurd
Too far-fetched to fucking believe
In Ealing within an hour of starting work
I bumped into Geordie Steve
I was doing surveys about Playstation 4
Respondent's got a five pound voucher for taking part
After eating a pastry from Gregs
I thought I should make a start
Who'd want to do my survey?
Who's got a spare ten minutes for a fiver
Aah some charity fund raisers
Perhaps one of them is a potential skiver
Perhaps one of them would be up for slopin off
To do my survey if I were them I would
The nearest one to me I approached
But how the hell really could
I have predicted that the one I approached
The one with old school slim shady hair
Be the Geordie from my past
Was this some fucked up mad nightmare?
See I didn't realise straight away
Cos it had been about ten years or so I can't remember
Since I'd last seen Geordie Steve
So why on this day on the 1st of fucking November
2013 in West London in Ealing
Why the fuck would our paths cross now
Holy fuck Bart Simpson
Eat my shorts I'm having a cow!
See he declined my invitation to do a survey
He said he was busy working

That he couldn't just go and do a survey
Cos his boss was lurkin
But what was unusual was his Geordie accent
And as I turned my back to walk away
The penny dropped, the face, the voice
The job he was doing, Geordie Steve, haway!
So I walked into TK Maxx
I was in shock, did that just happen? Surely not!
He must have recognised me
Surely my face he could not have forgot
I mean I haven't changed all that much
Yeah he knew it was me
But he must have been spun out too
I was probably the last person he expected to see
Especially when you consider I approached him
It was me that got all up in his grill
Ten years ago he'd wanted to stab me
Chucky from Childs Play kill kill kill!
Now out of nowhere here I was
Trying to talk to him in Ealing
As he turned and walked away I wondered
What the fuck was that Geordie feeling?
Was he feeling angry?
Was he feeling confused?
Was he feeling slightly nostalgic
About our friendship and all the hoes that we abused?
I was feeling fucking odd!
The whole situation was proper off key
I didn't know what to do
So I hid in a park behind a tree
Should I go and face him?
Try and front it, try to make friends
What would happen then though?
Would we make amends?
I mean I didn't actually fuck his ex
I could explain my version of events
But fucking hell dealing with this shit
Was proving far too intense

I decided I didn't want to make a decision
So I stayed in the park out of the way
I didn't know whether to speak to Steve
And if I did what would I say?
So rather than approach potential respondents
On Ealing Broadway with my colleagues in a team
I spent the day approaching people in a park
No way, no fucking way did I dream
That I'd be hiding from Geordie Steve
In case he was trying to find me and had a knife
As for the rest of the afternoon it's one big blur
What can I say, I guess that's just park life!!

Haway With The Cancer!

I'd had a fucked up first day in Ealing
Still I got to sleep ok
And when I woke up the next morning
I was stunned to find the lump on my ball had gone away
All that worry about my bollock lump
Well it had all been Geordie Steved
I'd been thinking about that Geordie so much
I forgot about my lump and boy was I relieved
To find the lump had fucking vanished
My faith in God restored
Thank you Geordie Steve you scared my lump away
And now I'm completely cured!!

Day 2 In Ealing!

It was my second day working in Ealing
I wondered if Geordie Steve would re appear
Fortunately I had a look out on my team
I'd had a quiet word in my colleague's ear
My friend Frank, my big buddy
I'd told him why I'd spent the previous day hiding
The history of me and Steve
And why I therefor was deciding
To remain fucking vigilant
So I gave Frank a thorough description of my northern foe
And told him if he saw him or someone that could be him
To find me quick and let me know
And would you Adam and Eve it
A little later that fucking morning
Frank came over and said "Is that him over there?"
"Fuck yes it is Frank thank you for that warning"
Then off I dashed back into Ealing Park
To hang out with my new friend a squirrel
I'm such a spineless jelly fish
My parents should have named me fucking Cyril
So yeah day two in Ealing was spent hiding in a park
Like a commando hiding from gooks in Vietnam
Why are you such a coward Fuzz?
I don't know you mother fukka I can't help it I just am!
Frank came and found me in the afternoon
To tell me Steve and his cohorts had definitely moved on
At last I could leave the park and show my face
The coast was clear, yes it was true
Geordie Steve had gone!!!

Let The Fuzz See The Fuzz!

I'd had enough of Ealing
I was sick to death of Ealing Park
I'd had enough of Geordie Steve
And all this hiding lark
So I was thrilled to be on my way to Shoreditch
To a pub called 'The Shoreditch'
To go see D.J. Fuzzilicous Fresh
The fuzzy D.J. bitch
I went and saw the fuzzsta
I'd not seen her in real life
She is a thing of beauty
She'll make someone a fuzztastic fucking wife
I got us a bottle of expensive bubbly
Very nice it was
I really should have stayed there longer
But I didn't and I left because
I'd decided I was gonna go meet Emma
In Vauxhall and go raving
I wasn't 100% convinced I'd actually do that
But I was now very drunk and misbehaving
I didn't want to be shitfaced pissed
And do something stupid around D.J. Fuzz
Just getting to meet her
Was for me a gigantic fucking buzz
So I figured I'd leave whilst things were peachy
It was probably just as well
I was far too drunk to go to Vauxhall
Instead I went back to Ealing Broadway
And back to my hotel!!

Fuzzilicous Fresh!

She's got big fuzzy hair
She's a top fucking D.J.
She's quite unique the fuzzy freak
And I think I'd have to say
That no other D.J. is as hot
She's way more fit than Annie Mac
D.J. Fuzzilicous Fresh in a low cut dress
Has something other D.J.'s lack
Sex appeal the sassy bitch
She's like a frizzy Carmen Electra
Fuzzy Fresh she's sure to impress
Next stop a residency on BBC Radio One Extra!!

Fucking Fat Hunchback!

I fucked this fucking fat hoe once
The hunchback tub of lard!
If I hadn't taken three Viagra's
I'd have never got my penis hard
I actually fucked this fucking fattopotamous
The Stacey Solomon sounding div
I could have wrote a longer story
But this is all the space I'm prepared to give
To the fat retarded fucking doughnut
As it was just a one night deal
This rhyme is quite sufficient you podgy slut
Unlike your super-sized McDonalds meal
Yeah you know you want that McFlurry too
Go on have that apple pie
I hope you're reading this you flabbersaurus
And I hope it makes you cry!!

Fats The Way I Like It!

That poem makes me sound like a cunt
I'm not fattest I love a squisher
And to the fat girl in that poem
Well in truth I'd like to wish her
All the best I don't hate her
If I saw her out I'd squeeze her chubby cheeks
I'm only pissed off cos when she mounted me
It fucked my back up and I couldn't walk for weeks!

G.I. Tyla!

Tyla was friends with Tom next door
In Chapel Square many years ago
Now he's an army marine
And he looks like G.I. Joe!!

Action Tyla!

On second thoughts not G.I. Joe
He looks like Action Man instead
One that likes abusing hoes
And shooting Afgans in the head!!

Lemonade!

Best Facebook message to a girl I ever sent
Was this . . . ok this is how it went . . . .
"Milk milk lemonade
I really want to bum you Jade!!"

Market Research

I still do market research
I'll do it until I'm retired
Or until I'm made redundant
Or until I'm fired!!

Czech Ya self Before Ya Wreck Ya self!

I'd just got back from London
I was in need of a Chinese whore
But when I phoned the number up
I found it weren't in use no more!
I tried once more just in case
The number still said not in use
No more Chinese brothel
Someone hand me a chair and noose
I can't go on without my Chinese brothel
I am contemplating suicide
Perhaps I had dialled the wrong number
So once again I tried
To get through but the number wasn't working
Maybe this was a temporary hic up
Yes I'm sure within a few days
They'll be more Chinese whores to stick my dick up
But I needed to fuck someone now
It'd been emotional seeing Geordie Steve and Fuzzilicous
A whore a day keeps the doctor away
And I wanted a fit blonde golden delicious
So I got on adultwork.com
I knew there were escorts local to me
Turned out there were quite a few
But the one I just had to go see
The one that was by far the sexiest
Was a stunning escort from Czechoslovakia
Sure there were a couple of English escorts near by
But fucking an East European would surely be wackier
So I phoned her up immediately
"Can I see you in an hour?" "Yes . . .
I live in Tankerton phone me when you're near
And I'll give you my address!"

I jumped into the shower
Gave my cock a wash
I thought I'd make the effort
Before I went off to get a nosh
The weather outside was frightful
Like that God awful Christmassy song
Fortunately Tankertons quite nearby
The trip wouldn't take too long
I jumped on a double decker bus
Ten minutes and I'd be there
I'd shaved my balls and everything
And put on my favourite underwear
I texted her to tell her I was on my way
She text me back her road and her house number
I really hoped she'd be up for anal
So I could leave saying I bummed her!
I found the house in no time at all
It was in fact a bungalow
I rang the doorbell then I waited
For my Czech Republic hoe
Wowzers what a stunner
Absolute porn star material
Lucky I'd had three Shredded Wheat
That morning for my cereal . . . .
Cos I'd be needing all my strength to fuck this lady
She was tall and had big tits
I didn't just want to fuck this hoe
I wanted to smash her cunt to bits
She was wearing a black silky robe
And she smelt so fucking sweet
She flashed me in the hallway
Her fanny looked good enough to eat
It was neatly shaven
And her clit was pierced with a silver ring
She had long brown hair and false eyelashes
She was a proper naughty thing
When we got into the bedroom
I got her to lay down

First I took my jeans off
Then I undid her silky gown
I wanted to lick her pussy
It was such a lovely pussy I had to lick it
She'd gone to the trouble of piercing her clit with a ring
So I used my tongue to flick it
I licked her pussy like a ninja
I wanted to make this Czech hoe cum intensely
When she started to dig her nails into my back
I knew she was enjoying it immensely
Then she cum and sprayed her whore juice
Right into my face
Being caked in dirty whore juice
Is to be honest fucking ace
I had a fucking hard on now
A right old fucking stonker
Time to use my Albert Wick, my dipstick
My rod you fucking plonker!
I lifted her legs onto my shoulders and stuck my cock in
After all this was costing me a lot of wonga
I pushed my dick in as far as it would go
Shame it's not a wee bit longer
Still I went for it with all my might
I drilled her pretty good
Then got her on all fours
Cos I decided I really should
Attempt to fucking bum her
She was East European after all
So I spat onto her ring piece
I did it all nonchalant and cool
Then I stuck one of my fingers in
Testing how far she'd let me go
But she went all Amy Winehouse
When sent to rehab and said "No no no!"
So I fucked her pussy from behind instead
Then got her to get on top
She rode me for a while
But then I instructed her to stop

I asked her to suck my cock for her grand finale
Her cock sucking was sublime
I was laying there like a fat roman emperor
I was having a thoroughly good time
She winked at me whilst deep throating
The naughty naughty fucker
She really was a fucking expert
Czechoslovakian cock sucker
I ejaculated into her mouth
She gargled it then went to the sink
And spat it out, washed it away
And poured herself a drink
I was cunt struck by this escort
I proposed right there and then
I quickly told her I was only joking
But that I'd be sure to visit her again
Then I put my shoes and socks on
And my jacket and gave her a kiss goodbye
I was grinning from ear to ear as I skipped off
Still buzzing from my dirty Czech hoe high!!

The Chinese Takeaway

I walked past the Chinese brothel one afternoon
And realised to my despair
That it had gone forever
Inside was completely bare
No more Chinese hookers
At least not from across the street
I've still got a Chinese takeaway though
So I can still get Chinese to eat
Just can't eat no Chinese pussy
Unless there's cat in their chop suey
Can't believe it's over, the brothels gone
No more Hong Kong foo'ey!

2nd Hand Crack Whores!

If you advertised that you love 3 toothed crack whores
3 toothed crack whores you'll start to attract
I'd been advertising that I loved toothless crack whores
Really I'm not lying that's a fact!
On Facebook I was always saying
That 3 toothed crack whores were my fave
I started messaging the ultimate 3 toothed crack whore
But she was already fucking my mate Pave
I didn't want to step on his toes
He's my pal so I did nuffin
But he mugged her off after a week or so
Cos she was a proper ragamuffin!
He then gave me the go ahead
Said she gave amazing head
But that she was shit in bed
And that I should have a wank instead
He told me she had proper dirty teeth
And that she had at least five missin
He said she was a weird one
And he still hadn't finished dissin
He said she didn't talk much
And her fanny was uncomfortably tight
She sounded perfect to me though
So I got her to come stay at mine that night!

Comic Relief Teeth!

You came to mine to get stoned
Messed up face just skin and bone
When did you have your last hot meal?
You look like a Comic Relief appeal
My charity case off Pave and Dappy
You best come in cheer up be happy
Sit down skin up, have a drink, get high
You're so small! I feel like a giant "Foe fum fee fi"
Right now you're high and drunk me too
I love 3 toothed crack whores I really do
Let's go to bed you undernourished fuck
Here's a penis for you to suck
Go ahead don't be coy
You've got no tits are you a boy?
Never mind I think you're fit
My cocks hard now, sit on it
I'm gonna fuck you all night you rancid hoe
Then in the morning you must go
Back home to your concentration camp
Cos you're a dirty skanky hood rat tramp!!

Bulimics and Anorexics!

Bulimics and anorexics keep fucking me
What the hell is up with that?
When I'm on top of them skinny bitches
I actually feel quite fat!!

Visual Aids

At first glance you appear ok
But now I've taken off my shades
I can see you only have about three teeth
And you look like you've got Aids!!

The Wrong Trousers!

I owned these smart grey trousers
They were really rather posh
But a little tight on the gonads
My nut sack they would squash
And one night after I'd worn them out
I instantly could tell
That their fucking tightness
Had caused my left nut to slightly swell
Then I had a flashback
That night at Folk Week I'd had them on
I never had cancer of the balls
It wasn't a tumour that had been and gone
It was just a swelling from squashing my testicle
When I'd sat cross legged on the beach
I obviously hadn't noticed the pain due to the M.D.M.A.
And I guess that'll fucking teach
Me for doing drugs in a Jesus t shirt
And using God's name in vain
The Lord all mighty squashed my nuts
As if to tell me don't you dare do this again
Sorry God, sorry Jesus
You scared me there for a bit
I really thought I had fucking cancer
That was some proper heavy shit
You've taught me that I was wrong
That I was a right old sod
Making fun of Mr Gnome's ball cancer
And taking drugs whilst preaching God
So here's a Hail Mary
And me saying Holy Father I repent
Damn those tight trousers straight to hell
And amen, thank Christ the swelling went!

Yellow Face

Seven years ago my mum and dad decided
To sell their house and land
To a building contractor
But first he needed permission for what he planned
That's planning permission der brain
Once he had that the deal was set in stone
Unfortunately what no one really expected
Was for the neighbours to kick off and moan
But that is what fucking happened
Dirty two faced jealous twats
It was only for a small four house development
Not a twelve story block of flats
The whole street signed a petition led by Yellow Face
A lizard cunt on the council's board of directors
This protest really put a spanner in the works
For the building firm, the potential house erectors
The council rejected the planned development
It then went to appeal
They also rejected planning permission
Unbelievable! Were my mum's neighbours actually for real?
I mean the fat hoe next door
Use to be all nicey nice
Now she'd become proper nasty
Well here's a free piece of advice
Karma is a mother fucker
Although you're one mum it wouldn't fuck
Karma probably wouldn't fuck your fat daughters either
But with any fucking luck
Karma will fuck your ginger husband
And your dopey looking son
Can't believe you turned so nasty
Well when all this is over and done
You'll still be fat and ugly
And your husband will still be ginger! So there!

The houses will still get built
You still won't like it and I don't care
As for you the other next door neighbour
I remember when my dad was dying
You sent an angry letter cos someone squashed your shrubbery
Well you're lucky your shrubs aren't fucking flying
Through your bloody letter box
You vile and rancid hag
Fuck you and your miserable life
You petty petulant old slag
The rest of the street are just as bad
And give or take the odd exception
Over the last thirty or so years
You've proved yourselves to be masters of deception
You know the type . . . nice as pie to your face
But really behind your back they plot to get you
You spineless gutless suburban fucks
When my mum moves I can't wait to forget you
You're everything I hate about perceived normality
You queen worshipping bunting lovers
I'm gonna miss you all about as much
As I miss my two half brothers
Anyway after six attempts to get it passed
The building contractor got the green light
For three bungalows to be built
Fuck you neighbours serves you right
Although despite planning permission being granted
Nothing's been built as of yet, it's still in limbo
Cos after all that palava
My mum got told just before last Crimbo
That the building contactor couldn't raise the funds
To buy her house and yard
What should've been a simple house sale and development
Is proving ridiculously hard
I should be lording it up right now on my private yacht
With my cut of my mums money
But what I'm most fucked off about
Is all this extra worry for my mummy

Although she says she's not that bothered
Like that comedian woman Katheryn Tate
It's almost as if the house doesn't want to be knocked down
Perhaps that is just not to be its fate
I don't know what'll happen
My mum might just stay for good
At least if she does it's now common knowledge
What I think of the cunts in her neighbourhood
I hope the fucking lowlifes read this
I doubt they will, not their cup of tea
They are way too lame
To ever read a book by Pimpydee
But if this is by some miracle one of you
Then ha! I just dissed you bad
I hope you take it personally
And I hope it makes you mad!
Yellow Face you lost we got planning permission
We overcome your dirty tricks
Even if the builder don't raise the money
You'll still be seeing bricks
I'll buy a fucking brick load
Then maybe I'll build those bungalows instead
Failing that I'll just put them through your window
Or throw them at your head!!

It's All Gone Pete Wrong!!

In my first book there's a rhyme or two about Pete
Which if you've read my first book you'll have seen
There's one about going clubbing with him
And one called A.T.M Nash Machine!
Peter is an awesome guy
Everything he's ever touched has turned to gold
And from my nights at Pete's in London
Lots of messy stories can be told!
Pete left London to live in Australia
He became Peter the ex-pat
His life, his job, even his belly
Had all become increasingly more phat
Obviously with Pete living in Australia
I very rarely get to see him
Apart from when he's back in England
Pete's so successful you feel like you want to be him
A week before Christmas Pete phoned me
I got a Pete call from fucking Oz
I felt quite privileged to get a call from Pete
Why had he phoned me? Well because
He was flying over to England for Christmas
To spend Christmas with his folks
But that he'd obviously want to see his pals
However it appeared this was all a hoax
Cos when it was almost Christmas
I'd still not seen or heard from Pete
I felt a little disappointed
Catching up with him is always neat
I wondered what had happened
But I didn't investigate
Then on the eve of Christmas Eve
I got a phone call from Steve my good mate
"Oh you might want to sit down for this
I've got some news that will blow your mind

Peter our friend Peters in custody in Australia
And if you type his name in Google you will find
That he got busted by the Australian feds
As part of a worldwide F.B.I. sting
Turns out Peter's allegedly the chief moderator
For a global drug black market website thing
If found guilty he faces extradition
And 25 years to life in a U.S. penitentiary!!"
"No fucking way! I don't believe it, can't be true!"
"Oh my dear Watson elementary
Check it out on the internet
Pete's on ABC fucking news!"
I checked it out it was true
Then I got the Pete's in jailhouse blues
How could this be possible
This wasn't like Pete he's far more wily
For forty fucking years
Pete's lived the life of Riley
And now he's in fucking prison
Pete and his poor parents must be going through hell
All we can do is hope and pray
This story somehow manages to end well
Pete's got a lot of amazing friends
Everyone's doing all they can
No one can believe this shit
The F.B.I. have obviously arrested the wrong man
Yet sadly as I sit writing this
Peter's still locked up
Either the F.B.I. have made a mistake
Or Pete really has cocked up
Unfortunately he can't discuss the case
So did he do it? I don't know!
Even if he's innocent he went straight to jail
Without collecting £200 or passing go!
If I win the lottery
I'll use my winnings to help him out
But until I win the Lotto I'm skint
So for now I can't do nowt

Darnel sanchez

Apart from write and send him letters
And hope they cheer him up a bit
Pete I love you dude
Can't believe this fucked up shit
Hopefully this will all get sorted out
And you'll be free soon that's what I hope!
In the meantime buddy I'll keep sending letters
Along with some soap . . . . on a rope!!!

Ass-Phyxiation

The Chinese brothel was closed down for good
The Czech hoe was gone and I was running out of whores
I only knew of one other fat one in Whitstable
Who to be honest I wouldn't have touched with yours
So in an act of hopeful desperation
I Google searched escorts in Whit-stable
Luckily it brought up interesting results
If it hadn't this would be one shit-fable
It brought up a Thai escort
Well what do you know!
Just when things looked bleak
I found yet another foreign hoe
I phoned up the Thai bird right away
She answered! I'd struck gold
"£60.00 for half an hour darling!"
"Fantastic, I'm in, no more bids, going going sold
I'll come see you at 8 pm!"
"Ok darling I live close to the tower block
Text me when you're near and I'll give you my address!"
"Did you hear that?" I asked my cock
"I'm taking you for a massage
A nice Thai massage as a treat
To make up for the last two months
Where you I've spanked and beat!"
I found the Thai birds apartment
Went into her bedroom and got naked
She stripped down to her bra and pants
And my £60 quid she take'ed!
This whore was what you'd expect
From a dirty Thailand hooker
Amazing body, big tits for an Asian
But facially not a looker

Her pussy was a decent pussy
A welcoming type of hole
So I stuck my face between her legs
And lapped at it like a cat lapping from a bowl
Then she sucked my ol' boy
In a Jimmy hat
Health and safety for all concerned
It's good that they do that
Then I shoved it in her fanny
Completely void of all emotion
My cock slipped up easily
Cos she'd caked her cunt in baby lotion
I fucked her doggy style for a bit
Then missionary, then we spooned
I stuck two fingers up her butt
That Thai hoe got harpooned
She didn't appreciate me doing that
"No anal sorry me no do!"
So I took my fingers out her arse
And stuck um in her foo!
I got the Thai bitch to ride me
So I could lay back and catch a breather
She gave my cock a Thai massage
With the walls of her Thai beaver
But my cock was being stubborn
I said "Oie come on mate
My half hours almost up
And you need to ejaculate"
The Thai whore began to wank me off
Her arse was in my face
Ass-phyxiation was an idea
I'd often been tempted to embrace
So I pulled her arse in closer
Gotta make the most of hoes
I cupped her pussy over my mouth
And in her bum hole I stuck my nose

Blocking all my airways
Through ass and muffication
Amazingly this felt fantastic
I really enjoyed this suffocation
Now I see why Michael Hutchence
Died wanking, naked, head in noose, asphyxiating!
Getting wanked off and blanking out
I was fucking really rating
Just before I passed out
I spunked in the Thai whores face
Ass-phyxiation might not be for everyone
But personally I'd say it's ace
My Thai hoe was very happy
That she'd helped me achieve my happy end
She said "Do you live local?
Cos I'd like you to be my friend!"
"Yeah I live just down the road
Sure I'll be friends with you
My name's Darnell Pimpydee Sanchez
A.K.A. Fuzzman how do you do!"
She was like "I live here on my own
I don't have friends, punters are all I see
We could go out for drinks
Or just hang out and watch a dvd!"
So that's how I befriended a Thai escort
Had she had a better face I'd have hung out with her for sure
But she didn't so I didn't
Still she was a friendly whore
So no doubt I'd go see her again
And maybe suffocate for a bit whilst she wanked me
Anyway I got dressed and as I left
She gave me a kiss goodbye and thanked me
I walked home feeling amused
Another East Asian slut I'd fucked
My cock was happy with his treat
He'd been massaged by a cunt and sucked

So yeah a good time was had by all
And I'd made a friend for life
One who I could use to Ass-phyxiate myself
No need for a Thai wife
Why bother marrying a Thai lady
When I can just see a Thai hooker instead
Just gotta make sure
I don't suffocate underneath the whore
And wind up fucking dead!!

Around The World In 80 Whores!

I've fucked a Filipino lady, a Korean girl
A hotty from Japan, a Thai and about 50 or so Chinese
I used a Johnny every time
I've not caught a sexually transmitted disease
I've fucked a lot of oriental bitches
No really! I've fucked a lot!
Some have been fucking ropey
But mostly they've been hot
I really did enjoy it
I've certainly had a lot of fun
I've fucked a girl of every nationality
From the land of the rising sun
So yeah that's some fucking achievement
That's a lot of East Asian holes
But what now what's next for me?
I need to set myself new goals
I'm thinking Europe should be my next challenge
I've only fucked 2 Swede's, a Czech and a Fin
That leaves a lot of European nationalities
I've yet to stick my willy in
Yeah some people go off and travel the world
Well they are welcome to their world tours
I'm gonna experience different languages and cultures
By fucking shit loads of foreign whores!!

The Forgotten Hoes

To all the hoes I fucked but never mentioned
You are the bitches I forgot
Don't take it personally I'm just forgetful
I can't help it I smoke pot!

Your Books All Sucked!

To all the sluts that gave me head
But never made my books do not despair
I've done this rhyme it's for all you swallowers
And you spitters and you with cum still in your hair!
I must have forgot your names and the time
Tick tock tick tock tick tock
I wish I could remember every dirty slag
That's ever sucked my cock!!

Funny As Fuck

For a chubby hairy ethnic
With no muscles and no car
I sure have bedded some beautiful girls
In fact I'd even go as far
As saying I've proven you can laugh a girl into bed
Even if she's smoking hot
Which is fucking lucky really
Cos a sense of humours all I got!!

What The Fuck Happened To Everyone??

Maybe some of you are wondering
What became of him or her
I could tell you but I'm not gonna
Cos I don't wanna so ner!
Oh ok I'll update you as best I can
Let's start with Kate my first ever girlfriend
Married, two kids, still tall, still fit!!
Jane? My daughters mum still drives me round the bend
She had another daughter with a dude called Luke
That relationship didn't work out well
What's she doing these days?
Is she single? Hard to tell!
She's just split up with someone
But I doubt she'll be single for long!
Chomps? Chompy lives in Australia
She pole dances in a thong!
Troll Face? I think she had a baby
With that Irish chap
She don't talk to me no more
Which is kinda crap!
Tufts? Found a long term partner
She's preggers now, congrats!
Fudgey? Has had a baby!
Man I guess my ex conquests all wanted brats!
Goldilocks? Yep she's pregnant too
She found a dude whilst my C.K. boxers aired!
K.Y.? Also pregnant, fucking hell
Have any bitches I've fucked been spared?
Well Slaps definitely hasn't had more kids
She don't talk to me now though!
Splodgey? The fake baby bitch
I presume she's still a fucked up Medway hoe!

Jenna? Fuck knows what happened to her
I know she had some kids with some man
I'd imagine her mum is still a smack head
Cos she was heroin's biggest fan!
What about your buddies? All settled down!
Ian and Amanda have a son and now a daughter on the way
Steve and Les (preggers) are engaged to be married
Chris? Well he's still gay!
Ok he's not! He's still with the Mumpsta
A.K.A. Tons of Fun
Martin and Natalie are still happily married
They've had a kid already and are expecting another one!
Trev's still with his missus
They apparently still fight and row
Last I heard she was also pregnant
And being a right stroppy cow!
Man, writing this is so monotonous
All this grown up shit's so depressing
Matt? Good ol' Matt's still single
And that's a fucking blessing
Cos if it weren't for him I'd have no wing man
Well I suppose there's always Dappy
He got big! He hit the gym!
Now he's always positive and happy
Got a lot of time for him
A proper decent guy
Ben? My Ben in Sweden, man,
His life story would make you cry
Talk about roller coasters
My Ben's had one crazy ride
Ups and downs highs and lows
After his divorce Ben began to slide
Rapidly into depression
Kat you ruthless whore
A month after your wedding
And you tell him you don't love him anymore
Well fuck you Kat Ben's a legend
And I'm very happy to say

Darnel sanchez

He's got a new Swedish bird
And he still lives in Sweden to this day!
Geordie Steve? Well it appears he's still alive!
Manchester Chris? Probably back on bail!
His brothers Dan and Phil are back in Manchester
And my mate Pete is still in jail!
And that is all I know I'm afraid
Sure there are other people in my books I've not included
That's cos I don't know what they're doing now
And that is the reason why they've been excluded
But to all of them and all my ex's
All my friends past and present
I wish you all the very best
I hope your lives are really pleasant
I don't wish bad on anyone
Even people that have done me wrong
If the world was full of people like me
Then everyone would get along
But it's not it's full of dickheads
Isn't that a fucking shame
Never mind they can't help being dickheads
They haven't worked out life's one big game
And that they are taking it too seriously
They should lighten up and have some fun!
Anyway I hope you found this rhyme informative
Cos that was the only reason it was done!

Final Whore!

I figured I'd go see my friend the whore
The Thai one with whom I'd become acquainted
The one who's arsehole and cunt I submerged my face in
Until I almost fainted!
My plan was simple, what I'd do
Was fuck her again whilst high
Then after invite her over to mine
And then attempt to try
To fuck her again for free
A free hooker, now that saves money
And well being friends with a hooker
Is let's face it pretty funny
But when I got to the hookers flat
She bamboozled me completely
"I've brought a friend to fuck you tonight!"
Then in came some new Thai hoe to meet me
Well I had not expected this!
This was just like the Chinese operation
Obviously this was a Thai brothel
That was the only obvious explanation
This new Thai whore had clearly been briefed
On what shananigans I would attempt
Most whores say no to anal
But of that this whore was exempt
Her opening sentence to me was this
"Darling I do anal, you cum in my face, I like!"
"Ok there's an extra £20 now just do it bitch!"
Damn I was so excited I became an advert for Nike
But to be honest it was all far too robotic
This was a hardened Thai whore vet
She lubed up her arsehole
And made it way too slippy and wet
I still bummed her! Fucking right I did!
Bumming is my speciality

It's not often though that I get to bum
Someone of a different nationality
So I bummed her but I didn't cum in her face
Cos I spunked in the Johnny prematurely!
The whole experience had been a let down
I was better than this! I had to be surely!
It dawned on me that I'd become addicted
To fucking escorts and brasses
I came to the conclusion that there must be more to life
Than paying to spunk up hookers arses
And that's when I made a vow
That would be my last ever paid for fuck
Never again will I pay prostitutes
My own dick I'll have to suck
I can't justify the financial cost
Plus I'm supporting an underground world of vice
Prostitution is morally wrong
Even though to every hooker I've been nice
So no more hookers from this point forth
I'm drawing a line in the sand
I'm sorry if you're a hooker and this upsets you
But I need you to understand
No matter how much you advertise
No matter how much I need a shag
I've made a promise to myself
To never again pay money for a slag!!!

Dear Marie In Case I Die!

Nothing in life is certain
Today I could get knocked down by a bus
Actually one thing in life is certain
And will happen to all of us
No one lives forever
Eventually we're all gonna die
But if that happens to me quicker than I'd like
Please don't be too sad, breakdown or cry
Cos I've lived my life and enjoyed it
I've got through it smiling and happy
And I want the same for you so here's some tips
On how to make your existence seem less crappy
Tip 1) don't take life too seriously
Tip 2) don't care too much what others think
Tip 3) do whatever makes you happy
Tip 4) it's ok to smoke, take drugs and drink
Tip 5) so long as you don't get addicted
Tip 6) be smart don't be a fool
Tip 7) don't let anyone put you down
Or bully you at all
Tip 8) show people the same respect that they show you
Tip 9) don't let love make you weak, stay strong
Tip 10) don't stay with someone that treats you bad
Tip 11) two wrongs just make a bigger wrong
Tip 12) be nice and kind to everyone
And they should be nice back
If they aint well fucking fuck um
They clearly aint worth Jack
Tip 13) remember your body is a temple
Feed it with healthy things and keep it fit
Fat people only get fucking fat
Cos they consume too much unhealthy shit
Tip 14) be nice to every living thing
Animals and birds

Tip 15) religion is found within
You don't need an old book full of words
I don't know if there even is a God
Life could be one big computer game
No one really knows what it is
But these tips will still work just the same!
Tip 16) try and make a difference to people's lives
You can do it in some way
I'm sure just a smile from your awesome face
Would help brighten up their shitty day
Tip 17) don't get controlled by fucking control freaks
They are the worst kinda people I have met
They can't deal with people being free
And they haven't realised yet
That they are the biggest victims
Controlled by the fear of losing control
Why would you want to control someone else
It's not right just search your soul!
Tip 18) don't get into a relationship with a gangster
It'll only end in tears
Tip 19) don't commit any stupid crimes
And get locked away for years
Tip 20) don't let anyone bring you down
With their negativity, moaning and complaining
People like that sap your life force
Trust me babe it's draining!
Tip 21) trust your instincts if it feels wrong it is
So act fast avoid the danger
Tip 22) don't drink any drinks
Given to you by a total stranger
Tip 23) don't be fooled by mainstream media
The news is just a mind programming show
The evil that controls the world
Is up to no good as by now I'm sure you know!
Tip 24) beware of fucking lizard people
I'm sure that they exist
Tip 25) don't wait until you're about to die
To write a bucket list

Write one whilst you're still young
A list of things in life you want to do
Then tick them off one by one
The way your life pans out is up to you
Tip 26) every action has a reaction
Every choice you make causes ripples
If you get drunk, drive a car, run over some kids
And turn them into cripples
You will have that on your conscience
And it's important to keep your conscience clean
Which is why you shouldn't hurt people
Or be nasty, bad or mean!
Tip 27) you can do anything if you put your mind to it!
Practice makes perfect, hard work pays off
Tip 28) don't smoke too many cigarettes
Or you'll get a smokers cough!
Tip 29) trust no one
Tip 30) clean your teeth twice a day
Tip 31) don't be afraid to speak your mind
And always mean whatever you have to say
Tip 32) work to live, don't live to work
Tip 33) always live in the now
Tip 34) don't let greedy hangers on
Milk you for money like a cow
Tip 35) don't be a follower
Don't follow the herd don't be a sheep
Tip 36) always try and get a minimum
Of seven hours sleep
Tip 37) write a book about your life
Then in a way you'll live forever
I wrote three books about my life in rhyme
Cos I'm really rather clever!
Tip 38) don't get pregnant until you're sure
That the baby's daddy is gonna make a decent dad!
Tip 39) every morning when you wake up
Wake up feeling glad
That you're alive and about to have another day
To have a positive impact on the planet

Tip 40) don't spend your whole entire life
Living in fucking Thanet
Tip 41) a little white lie now and again is ok
If it's to make people feel better in themselves
Tip 42) be honest with your kids
Tell them Santa's not real and neither are his elves
Tip 43) do not think expensive cars
And houses is what equates to wealth
A truly wealthy person has real friends
And a family that loves them all blessed with perfect health
Tip 44) if you are with someone just cos they're rich
Then darling that makes you a hoe!
Tip 45) try and focus on what's good in your life
If you are ever feeling down and low
Tip 46) don't find a negative in a positive situation
Instead try and find a positive in everything
Tip 47) don't forget to party
Tip 48) don't be afraid to dance and sing
Tip 49) life is just a crazy trip
So try and kick back enjoy the ride
Finally tip 50) the only regrets you'll have in life
Are from not doing things cos you were afraid to fail
So never tried!!
Anyway if by chance I got hit by a bus
And now I'm squashed and dead
At least I can rest in peace
Knowing by you this poem has been read!!

When I Die!

When I die I have the following request
At my funeral please can you make sure they play
'Don't Worry Be Happy'
And 'Always Look On The Brightside Of Life'
Got that? Good! Ok!

When I'm Dead!

Another request for my funeral
In case I happen to die
I'd like a sex cage coffin
And I'd like it carried by
Umpa Lumpas
Umpa lumpa dumpa dee dee
I wonder how many dwarfs
It will take to lift me!!

Outro

So the time has come to end the book
Time to bring the trilogy to a close
If you've read all three parts
Then you will have read about a lot of hoes
You'll have read about my childhood, my teenage years
And my escapades ripping off shops
You'll have read about my drug habit
And my run ins with the cops
But I'm almost 40 now
And my daughters in her final years of school
I've become a grown up, I'm all burnt out
I don't do much these days at all
So this is probably the last book I'll write
Ok I might do one more when I'm an O.A.P.
Until then I'll take things easy
I'll pass my torch to my Marie
No doubt she'll write a book when the time is right
When the time is right for her to write
In fact she's already started
And her rhymes are pretty tight
Maybe she'll follow in my footsteps
Although I don't think I need that kinda stress
Could she be the next Eminem a girl one
A Feminem? Well all the indications point to yes!
What will become of me? Who knows!
Will I actually marry an oriental bride?
I doubt I'll find anyone to marry!
Lord knows I've fucking tried
I don't mind being single
I'm happy being on my own
Let's face it eventually everyone
Will end up all alone!
I think I'll join a gym
Try n get a little bit buffer

Maybe I'll campaign against animal cruelty
I don't like seeing my fuzzy friends fucking suffer
Maybe I'll become a political activist
Or go off to Tibet and become a monk
Maybe I'll just stay indoors and wank
Until I drown in my own spunk
Whatever I do I'll do it well
I assure you take it from me
Your wordsmith, your poet, your lyrical fuzzball
Your author the one and only Pimpydee!!

The End

Wall Of Shame

I really don't want to leave out anyone
As this is the last time for a long time
That I'll be doing this so here we go
Mum, Dad, Zoe, Sadie, Phil, Laura, Liam, Sam,
Emily, Craig, Uncle Albert, Owen and Ryan,
And every member of the family tree living
Or dead you are my family and I love you!
To all my friends, Ben, Steve, Martin,
Chris, Matt, Trev, Ian, Lil Dan, Manchester
Chris, Danny, Wayne, Dappy, Pave, Tyla
I could go on and on but to all the
Amazing pals I've ever met, worked with,
Distanced myself from all of you you are
Fucking awesome! Ex's you know who you
Are I love you all! All the cool
Females I have yet to bum but who
Are fine examples of your specie I love you
Too! Rosie, Pollen, Angel,
Fuzzilicous, Crofty the sex giant, Donna
From the sweet shop, Suzie Lee, fans you
Two are my fans thank you, Dan and Carmen
My surrogates, Jamaican Paul, Ken, Foxy,
My weed man, Dave, all the people that
Ever gave me a job, Pete free the Petey one!
Sucky Sue, Sue Two she's typing this B.T.W.
All my friends missuses, all the whores
Of the world, drugs I'd like to thank drugs
And alcohol for all the good times and lastly
My amazing best friend my daughter Moofsta xx.

About the Author

Having already published 2 autorhymeograhys the third was always a case of when not if, and here it is, the autorhymeography part 3, 'DIRTY SEX RAINBOWS . . . This book continues where FIFTY FEELS OF FUZZ left off, its the continuing story of DARNELL pimpydee SANCHEZ . . . a.k.a FUZZMAN . . . I am still the same guy who wrote the last 2 books and I still live in the same place, bingo bongo lets do this!!